STEFAN DUDRA

LEMKO IDENTITY AND THE ORTHODOX CHURCH

CARPATHIAN INSTITUTE

HIGGANUM, CONNECTICUT

2018

Lemko Identity and the Orthodox Church

By Stefan Dudra

Published by: Carpathian Institute, The Lemko Association, 184 Old County Road, Higganum, Connecticut 06441-4446 USA, www.lemkoassociation.org.

ISBN 978-1-938292-12-5

A previous edition of this book was published as *Sketches from the history of religion and identity of Orthodox Lemkos* (ISBN 978-0-692-58562-7) with the statement:

This publication is part of research conducted at the Department of International Relations of the Institute of Political Science at the University of Zielona Góra. Translation of this book was co-financed by Institute of Political Science at the University of Zielona Góra.

Translation (original edition): Jarosław Chojak, Arkadiusz Tyda
Technical editing (original edition): Jan Skowroński
Cover design (original edition): Arkadiusz Tyda
Editing and translation (revised edition): Paul J. Best, Michael Decerbo
Design and production (revised edition): Andrew Best, Michael Decerbo
Illustrations: Oil paintings on Lemko themes, possibly by N.A. Tsislyak. From the Carpathian Institute collections, unknown dates.

Library of Congress Control Number: 2018964957

Publisher's Cataloging-in-Publication Data

Names: Dudra, Stefan, author. | Best, Paul J. (Paul Joseph), 1939- editor, translator. | Decerbo, Michael, editor, translator.
Title: Lemko identity and the Orthodox Church / Stefan Dudra ; [editing and translation: Paul J. Best, Michael Decerbo].
Other Titles: Sketches from the history of religion and identity of Orthodox Lemkos
Description: [Revised edition]. | Higganum, Connecticut : Carpathian Institute, 2018. | Previously published as: Sketches from the history of religion and identity of Orthodox Lemkos. Translated from an unpublished Polish language text. | This work was based on both the previously published English language version and the unpublished Polish language text. | Includes bibliographical references and index.
Identifiers: ISBN 9781938292125
Subjects: LCSH: Lemky--Ethnic identity. | Lemky--Religion. | Orthodox Eastern Church. | Lemky--Politics and government. | Central Europe--Politics and government. | LCGFT: Essays.
Classification: LCC BR957.L46 D84 2018 | DDC 274.43082--dc23

Church in Tylicz, Nowy Sacz County

Church in Leszczyny, Gorlice County

Contents

Preface

When Prof. Stefan Dudra of Zielona Góra (Green Mountain) University in Poland sent us a copy of his *Sketches from the History of Religion and Identity of Orthodox Lemkos* (2017) our first impression was that the title seemed to be unusually formulated and the English language of the main text somewhat nonstandard. Yet after reading through the 132 pages of text it was clear to us that the book was remarkably meritorious as to content and, if the author would allow it, with judicious revision to the English and some inserted explanatory information it would be a singular addition to the ongoing debate concerning Samuel Huntington's *Clash of Civilizations* concept, and a valuable addition to the Carpathian Institute's *A Carpathian Library* series. The author agreed to let us work on his book and we are grateful.

The writer details the situation of those Lemkos who chose an Eastern Orthodox Christian position to defend themselves against the crushing force of Polish and Ukrainian (and, from the south, Slovak) nationalism. The reader may wish to note that that "Russian" nationalism is not dealt with in Prof. Dudra's book because while "Russophilism" (aligning with the Great Russian nation and state in various ways) was popular in the Lemko homeland to as late as 1944, since then, due to the depredations of the Red Army and the Soviet NKVD and the imposition of communism is Central Europe, Russia has fallen out of favor. Russia is still popular among some Lemko descendants in North America.

Following the rise of nationalism in the late 19th century, in the Lemko Region of the 1890s there arose a three-way struggle between Ukrainophiles (those who favored the Ukrainian national idea); the "Old Rus'", who identified with a general idea of *Rus'*— that all East Slavs (in the 21st century we would say, Great Russians, Little Russians/ Ukrainians, Belarusians and Carpatho-Rusyns) ought to have a common culture and religion; and the stark "Russophiles" who identified with Imperial Russia and the Tsar. Russophiles condemned the Ukrainians as "splittists"/"separatists" and later, as the Carpatho-Rusyn/Lemko-Rusyn idea developed, the Ukrainians blamed the Lemkos as separatists too, but this time in relation to the Ukrainian cause.

This struggle stretched all across the social spectrum but was particularly acute in the sphere of religion What had happened was this: in the 16th and 17th centuries some bishops of existing Eastern Rite dioceses switched jurisdiction from the Metropolitan of Kyiv and the Patriarch of Constantinople to the Metropolitan of Lviv and the Patriarch of Rome. About that same time a Patriarchate was established in Moscow and that office began to claim the allegiance of all Eastern Rite Slavic speakers in Central and Eastern Europe. Eventually two full scale Greek/Byzantine rite Catholic Churches were established, one in Lviv (also known as Lvov, Lwow, Lemberg or Leopolis) and one in Mukachevo/Uzhgorod. The Lviv jurisdiction, which covered all of the Lemko Region, eventually became identified with Ukrainian nationalism.

Note that the shift from Constantinople to Rome occurred way above the heads of ordinary believers. At least in the Lemko area, though not in other places, the people were not "forced" into the Unia (Union with Rome); it is doubtful they ever knew it had happened. The term *pravoslavny* ("correct worshippers"; that is, orthodox worshippers) continued to be used by all Lemkos. It was not like France under Louis XIV who revoked the Edict of Nantes (the edict which allowed the existence of Protestant Huguenots) and sent heavily armed "Dragoons" into Protestant houses of worship to "convert" the people back to Catholicism or to drive them out of the country.

No, the problem in the Carpathians began at the turn of the 20th century, when the seminaries in Lviv and Przemysl began to ordain aggressive Ukrainian nationalists to the priesthood, some of whom were celibate, an unusual thing among Lemko clergy. Lemkos were noted for their conservatism and their attachment to their rituals and customs, including bearded, married priests, with the priest's wife playing an important role in village life. So, when Ukrainian nationalist priests showed up, sometimes without a wife and sometimes shaven, and began to use the Ukrainian language in speaking and to preach about Ukraine and to have the Ukrainian Tryzub (trident) flag in church, they frequently met with resistance. Many believers, before and after WW I, turned to the Orthodox jurisdiction to preserve what they had received from their fathers (and mothers). Lemkos in North America also wanted to retain their heritage, and they found a willing partner in the Russian Orthodox Mission in

America which opened its arms to the newcomers. Note, there were no "conversions"— rather, there was switching of jurisdictions in order to save and keep an inheritance. The introduction of Ukrainianism, in effect, pulled the rug out from under traditional believers, who struggled to retain traditions.

But perhaps we have gone too far afield, let us return to Professor Dudra's book.

There is a trap for the unknowing in the use of the English term "Orthodox". As aforementioned, the broadest term used by all Slavic Eastern Rite Christians from Central and Eastern Europe was *pravoslavny* (correct worshiper)— in English the Greek-rooted word for correctness in worship is "Orthodox", thus we have Orthodox Christians, Orthodox Jews and even Orthodox Presbyterians. In North America the non-Catholic Eastern Rite Christians use "Orthodox" while those under Roman jurisdiction in North America (the Catholic Church recognizes sixteen rites besides the Latin rite, and the Slavonic "Greek" or Eastern Rite is fully accepted) use "Greek-Catholic" or "Ukrainian Catholic" or "Byzantine Catholic", but in the Lemko Region the term *pravoslavny* was used in services by both. Aggressive Ukrainian nationalist priests, actually against the orders of their hierarchs, began to use *pravoverny* (true believing) or even *katolitsky* in services, replacing *pravoslavny*.

Those who resisted this change and others eventually went over to the "Polish Autocephalic Orthodox Church", a semi-autonomous branch of the Moscow church, while south of the Carpathian crest they went to the Orthodox Church of Czechoslovakia. Lest one believe this is all anti-Ukrainian Lemko "separatism" this writer had occasion to speak with the late Bishop Adam, of the Orthodox Przemysl-Nowy Sacz diocese, who was resident in Sanok and his auxiliary bishop Pajseusz, resident in Gorlice. They both said they were Ukrainians, but "not that kind" which this writer took to mean, moderate — not aggressive. In fact when Bishop Adam was asked about side alars and statues of the Virgin Mary in his cathedral (both unusual in a standard Orthodox church), he said if the believers were used to them that he had nothing against it — that he was not a fanatic.

A more recent phenomenon in the homeland and in the Western and Northern Poland Lemko diaspora is about preserving and developing a

Lemko-Rusyn nation. Of particular interest is an article by Marta Watral, "What is Lemko Revitalization" which appeared in the Polish periodical *Znak* (No. 717, February, 2015) and which was translated into English and published in *Karpatska Rus'* (No. 1&2, 2017, p.15-16). The idea of a separate Carpatho-Rusyn nation is not new; see the book *Simeon Pyzh's 1938 Short History of Carpathian Rus'* published by the Carpathian Institute and the Lemko Association (USA) in 2016.

A few last notes in regard to terms before the main text begins:

Church - In some Slavic languages *cerkiew/tserkov* is used for any Eastern Rite church while *kostel/kosciol* refers to Western rite churches whether Catholic or Protestant; *templum* (temple) could be any number of things. All these are translated here as "church" or "house of worship".

Thalerhof - is the correct German spelling of the village where the internment camp of the same name was. There are a number of odd versions of Thalerhof about, but the original spelling should be used.

Sandovich - Finally, while there is a great deal said about Maxim Sandovich as a priest-martyr and lately a Saint in the Polish Autocephalic Orthodox Church, there were two other Sandoviches shot at about the same time for the same reason as St. Maxim: the Greek Catholic priest and dean of the Muszyna District, Piotr Sandovich and his student son Antoni. We never hear anything these two martyrs, nothing at all from anybody.

In regard to the term "deportation", it should be mentioned that this is a legal term, referring to putting someone over an international border to a foreign state (Americans are very aware of this meaning in regard to the deportation of illegal aliens) while resettlement/forced resettlement/forced dislocation in regard to Lemkos after 1947 refers to a change of residence within the borders of Poland.

Finally, while Prof. Dudra's original main text was adjusted to the demands of standard English the footnotes were not touched. These are a remarkable set of 379 references, quite comprehensive in scope, which are there for specialists who may want to do further research into Prof. Dudra's narrative. "The List of Sources and Literature" was also not modified that much.

Any comments, remarks, additional information, etc., would be gratefully received.

Paul J. Best, Ph.D.
Director, The Carpathian Institute
President, The Lemko Association (*Lemko-Soyuz*), USA
Series Editor of "A Carpathian Library"

Introduction

The subject of the Lemko people fascinates researchers because of their distinct material culture, rituals and tragic recent history. Issues associated with this population are of interest to historians, sociologists and ethnographers, as well as people who want to learn about the Lemkos and their "country" — Lemkovyna. For Lemkos their land was a "little homeland" filled with mountain landscapes. Its inhabitants lived there for generations.

However, Lemkovyna meant not just a certain territory, but the sum of its history, which consisted of tradition and religious and cultural heritage. A sense of connectedness, unifying and integrating all of these into one body, came into existence there. Important elements in preserving Lemko identity were both the Orthodox and Greek Catholic churches. Besides religious activities they filled important functions of creating and integrating culture. In difficult periods of history, it was possible to rebuild religious life and societal organization from scratch around the Orthodox and Greek Catholic churches.

I would like to devote considerations to issues concerning ethnogenesis of Lemkos, the origin of the name "Lemko", and Lemko territory. They will be supplemented by events related to the "disintegration" of Lemkovyna that occurred as a result of forced displacement in the years 1944-1947 [and later].

The Ethnogenesis of Lemkos

The question of the origin of the Lemko population remains a contentious one among scholars, as it is difficult to explain given the present state of research[01]. Basically, one can identify several theories. The domi-

---

[01] It is analyzed by H. Duć-Fajfer, Łemkowie w Polsce, "Magury 91", p. 16-18; T. A. Olszański, Geneza Łemków – teorie i wątpliwości, "Magury 88", p. 18-43, see also: J. Czajkowski, Studia nad Łemkowszczyzną, Sanok 1999, p. 111-146; M. Parczewski, Geneza Łemkowszczyzny w świetle badań archeologicznych, [in:] Łemkowie w histo-

nant theories are the indigenous[02] theory and the migratory (Vlach or Wallachian)[03] theory. According to the first, Lemkos are descendants of the tribe of White Croats, which was a part of Kyivan Rus'. Among other things, Ukrainian and Russian researchers indicate that initially a large part of the Carpathians was inhabited by a Ruthenian element. Lemkos are thought to have a pre-Slavic origin. After the fall of Kyivan Rus', and under the onslaught of the Tatars and Polish colonists, this population managed to survive in inaccessible mountainous areas[04].

According to the assumptions of the migratory theory, Lemkos represent a population resulting from the imposition of a Wallachian-Ruthenian wave of settlement on an earlier Polish settlement (existing since the thirteenth century). As a result of the movement of the Balkan pastoral tribes, the so-called Vlachs, the process of mixing with the population of the territory of the Western Carpathians came about[05]. It should be emphasized that according to [the Polish scholar] Roman Reinfuss this wave of Vlach-Ruthenian settlement consisted of two independent trends: an earlier one, probably dating back to the thirteenth century and made up of Balkan shepherds and nomads, and a later one in the form of Rus' [East Slavic] agricultural settlements from the fifteenth and sixteenth centuries[06]. As a result of an assimilation process, fusion of the Vlachs with the earlier and later agricultural settlement into homogeneous groups of highlanders came about. As a result of these processes Lemkos became the westernmost group of Rusyn-language followers of the Eastern Church[07].

---

rii i kulturze Karpat, red. J. Czajowski, Rzeszów 1992, part. 1, p. 11-25.

[02] Most Ukrainian and Russian researchers are supporters of the indigenous theory.

[03] Czech, Romanian and Polish researchers (K. Dobrowolski, R. Reinfuss) dominate among the supporters of this theory.

[04] See: I. F. Lemkin, Istorija Lemkowyny, Yonkers, N.Y. 1969, p. 40; I. Krasowski, Problem autochtonizmu Rusinów w Beskidzie Niskim, [in:] Łemkowie w historii i kulturze Karpat ..., p. 381-387.

[05] K. Dobrowolski, Migracje wołoskie na ziemiach polskich, Lwów 1930; idem, Z badań nad zagadnieniem wołoskim w Karpatach Zachodnich, [in:] Pasterstwo Tatr Polskich i Podhala, vol. VIII, Wrocław-Warszawa 1970, p. 131-164; A. Fastnach, Osadnictwo Ziemi Sanockiej w latach 1340-1650, Wrocław 1982; J. Czajkowski, Dzieje osadnictwa historycznego na Podkarpaciu i jego odzwierciedlenie w grupach etnograficznych, [in:] Łemkowie w historii i kulturze Karpat ..., p. 27-166.

[06] R. Reinfuss, Związki kulturowe po obu stronach Karpat w rejonie Łemkowszczyzny, [in:] Łemkowie w historii i kulturze Karpat ..., p. 168.

[07] T. A. Olszański, op. cit., p. 21. About the research on Wallachian colonization see: K. Wolski, Stan polskich badań nad osadnictwem wołoskim na północ od Karpat, "Rocznik Przemyski", 1958, p. 211-225; J. Nalepa, Łemkowie, Wołosi i Biali Chorwaci. Uwagi dotyczące kwestii genezy osadnictwa na polskim Podkarpaciu, "Acta

Bohdan Struminski criticized the Wallachian theory. He also rejected the autochthonity of Lemkos in the Beskid Mountains, and he derives their origin from the valley of the river Tisza in Subcarpathia (near the town of Khust). From there they moved to the Prešov region around the thirteenth century, and during the reign of King Kazimierz Wielki (1333-1370) to the northern side of the Carpathians[08].

The unexplained problem of Lemko origins has led to the construction of various new theories as well. Tadeusz Sulimirski derived their origin from a Dacian-Thracian tribe inhabiting the Carpathian Mountains in prehistoric times (i.e. the Thracian theory)[09].

Creators and supporters of various theories of the origin of the Lemko people consider them to be contradictory. However, as rightly observed by Zofia Szanter, these theories are mutually complementary. "Different tribes had been going to the mountains since prehistoric times; the settlement was multiwaved and virtually each observation reveals another piece of history: there were Thracians, Dacians, Celts, Croats, Polish settlers, the peoples of the Balkans and Rusyns"[10].

The dispute over the origin of the Lemkos has continued to this day. The arguments in favor of specific theories are not fully based on a scientific foundation and still await further research. Among others, the causes of Vlach migrations and the ethnic composition of Vlachs require explanation. As Tadeusz Andrzej Olszański claims, the "high degree of emotional involvement in this dispute of Lemko, as well as Polish and Ukrainian researchers and publicists is a problem"[11].

The Name

The terms "Lemko" and "Lemkos" emerged in history in the first half

---

Archeologica Carpathia", 1997-1998, vol. 34, p. 135-173.
[08] Z. Szanter, Osadnictwo z południa w Beskidzie Niskim i Sądeckim, "Polska Sztuka Ludowa", XXXIX, no 3-4, Warszawa-Wrocław 1985, p. 188.
[09] See: T. Sulimirski, Trakowie w północnych Karpatach i problem pochodzenia Wołochów, "Magury 85", p. 3-27. One of the most debated theories formulated by Paweł Szafarzyk, who presented the Lemkos as descendants of Sarmatian tribe Servi Limigantes who inhabited the Carpathians between 1st and 3rd century AD, see: P. Szafarzyk, Slovanskie Starožitnosty, Praha 1837, p. 210.
[10] Z. Szanter, Skąd przybyli przodkowie Łemków? O osadnictwie z południowych stoków Karpat w Beskidzie Niskim i Sądeckim, "Magury 93", p. 7.
[11] T. A. Olszański, op. cit., p. 18.

of the nineteenth century. It was probably used for the first time by Josyf Lewicki[12]. Previously, the inhabitants of the Beskid Niski and Sądecki were called "Rusnaks" or "Rusyns". The name "Lemko" initially had a pejorative meaning— some Ruthenians overused the word *lem* ("but", "only"). It made its way into literature and history from the second half of the nineteenth century[13]. A. I. Toroński stated that "The nickname 'Lemko' comes from the word *lem*, which they use in terms of Russian *lich* or Polish "but". The word *lem* is of Slovak origin and no other Rusyns but Lemkos use it [...] In their own language Rusyn-Lemkos never called themselves Lemkos, just straight Rusnaks, and not all of them know that nickname that only other Rusyns use"[for them][14].

Helena Duć-Fajfer rightly notes that the name was almost unknown among the Lemko population till World War I. It was not until the interwar period, which for Lemkovyna was a time of emerging ethnic consciousness, with a clash of different orientations and general political activity, that the term "Lemko" became widely used among Lemko activists. Roman Reinfuss stressed that the name "Lemko", which in ethnographic literature had a scientific importance, had a political coloration among Lemkos. This mainly refers to the central and western Lemko region, where Lemko separatism began to crystallize on the background of the political quarrel between the "Old Ruthenians" and "Ukrainians"[15]. In the aftermath of World War II, deportation to the USSR (1944-1946) and the forced resettlement of Operation "Vistula" (1947) the names "Lemko" and "Lemkos" almost completely replaced the terms "Rusnak" and "Rusyns".

Territory

Until the second half of the 1940s Lemkos lived in the territory called in Polish *Łemkowszczyzna* (Lemkivshchyna), and in Lemko *Lemkiwszczyzna* or locally, *Lemkovyna*. It covered the northern and southern slopes of the Carpathian Mountains, lying in Poland and Slovakia. Ties between

---

[12] J. Lewicki, Grammatik der ruthenischen oder kleinrussichen Sprache in Galizien, Przemyśl 1834. Wincenty Pol used it in that period, see: W. Pol, Rzut oka na północne stoki Karpat, Kraków 1851.

[13] S. Udziela, Rozsiedlanie się Łemków, "Wisła", 1889, vol. 3; R. Reinfuss, Łemkowie jako grupa etnograficzna, Sanok 1998, p. 16-17.

[14] Cit. from R. Reinfuss, Łemkowie jako grupa etnograficzna..., p. 17.

[15] R. Reinfuss, Łemkowie jako grupa etnograficzna..., p. 18.

populations living on both sides of the mountains were strong. They involved both language, and material and spiritual culture[16]. However, the following discussion considers only Lemkovyna on the north side of the Carpathians. I identify this area as the territory bounded on the east by the watersheds of the Osława and Laboretz rivers, and on the west by the Poprad River. The length of this wedge is approximately 150 km long and 60 km wide at its base. The Lemko village situated furthest west is Osturňa (on the southern side of the Carpathians) while on the north side, the Polish side, the westernmost part of Lemkovyna is called "Szlachtowska Ruś" which comprises the four villages in the Szczawnica area: Biała Woda, Czarna Woda, Jaworki and Szlachtowa[17].

At the dawn of Polish statehood, the area later known as Lemkovyna partially belonged to the tribe of Vistulans. Then, from the end of the reign of Mieszko I [A.D. 992] it together with the whole of Małopolska became a part of the Polish state. The first permanent settlements in the area of the Beskid Niski and Sądecki (the future Lemko region) were based on Polish common law. Then, in the fourteenth and fifteenth centuries, an increasing number of villages and towns were located there under the economically more efficient German law, and later under Vlach Law. In the sixteenth century most of the extant villages of later Lemkovyna were built[18]. It follows that the process of settlement in the area lasted several centuries, with a Lemko community created at its base. [A discussion of Polish, German and Vlach law is too large to insert here.]

The problem of the territorial boundaries of Lemkovyna has caused a lot of controversy and scientific debate. Various hypotheses have been put forward, particularly concerning the eastern borders of Lemkovyna. They were placed on the rivers Jasiołka or Wisłok, and even on the line of the upper San (by among others W. Pol and A. I. Toroński). Finally, in the 1930s as a result of interdisciplinary research by linguists and ethnographers (among others J. Szemłej, Z. Stieber, R. Reinfuss) the extent of the

---

[16] See: R. Reinfuss, Związki kulturowe po obu stronach Karpat w rejonie Łemkowszczyzny, [in:] Łemkowie w historii i kulturze Karpat ..., p. 167-181.

[17] H. Duć-Fajfer, Literatura łemkowska w drugiej połowie XIX i na początku XX wieku, Kraków 2001, p. 7; B. Horbal, Lemko Studies: A Handbook, New York 2010, p. 39-47.

[18] T. M. Trajdos, Osadnictwo na Łemkowszczyźnie, "Magury 90", p. 24-27. More about aspects of settlement and location of each village also: A. Fastnach, Osadnictwo ziemi sanockiej w latach 1340-1650, Wrocław 1962; J. Czajkowski, Studia nad Łemkowszczyzną, Sanok 1999.

Lemkovyna was determined "on the northern slopes of the Carpathian Mountains from the Poprad river on the west to the Great Watershed which demarcates the upper catchment of Osława and Solinka"[19] [on the east]. The western boundary is designated by the already mentioned "Szlachtowska Rus".

In the interwar period the area of Lemkovyna was 2136.63 square kilometers. On its territory there were 187 settlements, including approximately 170 inhabited almost exclusively by the Lemkos. The size of individual villages varied from small (eg. Smereczne - 2.97 km²) to large (eg. Bartne - 19.74 km²), but basically, small or very small villages dominated[20]. Administratively, during the 1920s Lemkovyna was divided into the districts of Nowy Targ, Nowy Sącz, Grybów (existing until 1932), Gorlice, Jasło, Krosno and Sanok[21]. During this period, the population was estimated in the range of 100-150 thousand. According to studies of the 1931 Polish census, the total number of Lemkos there at that time amounted to 130,121 people[22].

"Disintegration" of Lemkovyna. Dislocations from the years 1944-1947

The end of World War II was the beginning of an ordeal for the Lemko people. With the nascent communist system they were subjected to forced deportation and resettlement, initially, to the USSR (1944-1946), then as part of the Operation "Vistula" to the so-called Recovered Territories (1947)[23]. [Remnants were resettled as late as 1952.]

[19] R. Reinfuss, Łemkowie jako grupa etnograficzna, Sanok 1998, p. 19-24, see also: J. Szemlej, Z badań nad gwarą łemkowską, "Lud Słowiański", 1934, vol. 3, part. 2, p. 162-163; Z. Stieber, Wschodnia granica Łemków, "Sprawozdania z Czynności i Posiedzeń PAU", 1935, vol. 40, no 8, p. 246-249.
[20] However, due to fact that Muszyna and Jaśliska were purely Polish towns, 30.61 km² should be subtracted from the area, see: J. Czajkowski, Studia nad Łemkowszczyzną..., p. 162-163.
[21] K. Z. Nowakowski, Sytuacja polityczna na Łemkowszczyźnie w latach 1918-1939, [in:] Łemkowie w historii i kulturze Karpat..., p. 323.
[22] Data from: H. Duć-Fajfer, Literatura łemkowska w drugiej połowie XIX i na początku XX wieku..., p. 8. J. Czajkowski gives the number of 103,319 people, of which approx. 4,000 Poles and approx. 3300 Jews should be subtracted, see: J. Czajkowski, Studia nad Łemkowszczyzną ..., p. 173, 185. According to Fr. W. Maściuch there were 151 thousand Lemkos (including 131,984 Greek Catholics) in 1932, B. Maściuch, Pro Lemkiwszczynu, "Niwa", 1934, no 3, p. 83-87.
[23] So-called Recovered Territories are the areas of Western and Northern lands given

Deportations to Soviet Ukraine were made on the basis of the treaty of 9 September 1944 signed between the Government of the Ukrainian Soviet Socialist Republic and the Polish Committee of National Liberation (PKWN). On its basis a "right to resettlement" was granted to Ukrainians who held Polish citizenship as of 17 September 1939, and who after the signing of the treaty lived in the regions of Cracow, Rzeszów and Lublin (this also included Belarusians and Russians living in the area). The concept of "Polish citizens of Rus' nationality" was also introduced in the treaty. This concerned residents of Lemkovyna and Boykivshchyna of Greek Catholic or Orthodox faith who did not identify themselves with Ukrainian nationality [that is, the operative concept was that all East Slavs should move East]. Under the assumption that the "evacuation" (a term used in official documentation) was to be voluntary, without direct or indirect coercion, the basis for the resettlement were lists on which the names of people declaring their intention to leave Poland were inscribed. Declarations may have been made orally or in writing; in the former case unlimited possibilities for fraud were created[24].

Officially, the deportations started on 15 October 1944 and ended on 15 June 1946; in fact the whole operation was carried out until the end of 1946. Due to the avoidance of resettlement by many, despite statements about its voluntary basis Polish authorities began by mid-1945 to exert pressure in order to increase the number of applicants to leave Poland, using taxes or requisitions and conscription into forced labor [25]. Using troops, the authorities also began forced displacement of

---

to Poland after World War II.

[24] *Repatriacja czy deportacja. Przesiedlenie Ukraińców z Polski do USRR 1944-1946. Dokumenty 1944-1945*, ed. E. Misiło, Warszawa 1996, vol. 1, p. 9-10. In addition, the treaty contains information concerning, among others placing displaced persons throughout Ukraine in accordance with their wishes (on the kolkhoz farm or on the individual farm). There were applied concessions for those leaving Poland (including the cancellation of all tax arrears, relief from taxes and insurance) and it was determined what they could and what they could not take with them. Organization of evacuation was determined, its agents and representatives. In addition the executive instructions and complementary were issued to the treaty to lay down in detail mode, course and organization of deportations, see idem, p. 30-38; 45-59; 73-78; 296-297.

[25] Archives of New Files (AAN), The Main Representative of the Government Affairs for Evacuation in Lublin, sign. 166, The protocol of the meeting held in the district office in Gorlice on the expulsion of Lemkos to the USSR of 3 August 1945. The county executive of Nowy Sącz J. Łabuz's report was characteristic. He stated in information to the Chief Representative of the Government of Poland for Evacuation:

the population. They "pacified" [ethnic] Ukrainian villages, committing acts of violence, humiliation and murder against civilians[26].

In total, during this operation approx. 482,000 people (including more than 70,000 Lemkos) were displaced [27], including approximately 15,000 Orthodox from Lemkovyna[28]. It is difficult to determine how many Lemko people voluntarily went to Ukraine (among others, Lemkos of Biała Woda, Jaworki and Szlachtowa filed declarations of this type), and to what extent departures were coerced. Julian Kwiek rightly concludes that, in general, people did not want to leave their villages, and the authorities themselves noticed that they referred unfavorably to resettlement on Soviet territory. Analyzing the Lemkos' attitude to resettlement, Andrzej Kwilecki insisted that the population from areas affected by the war and poor people, hoping to improve their fate, left voluntarily. Others left in compliance with directives from authorities[29]. It seems that mainly attachment to one's place of birth, the feeling of being "at home", prevailed. Lemkos already knew the reality of life in the Soviet Union. They were aware that "sausages don't hang on fences there" (referring to claims made in propaganda encouraging Lemko people to travel to "rich" Ukraine).

At reluctant to go I put in 100% required to make a quota and any other benefits, the effect is that the population is they would submit all the benefits at 200%,, if only not to go, Repatriacja czy deportacja..., p. 274.

[26] The murder of the Ukrainian population had already begun in the first months of 1945. According to Grzegorz Motyka from 2600 to 3900 Ukrainians living in the border zone from Lubaczów to Sanok were killed in the period see. G. Motyka, Tak było w Bieszczadach. Walki polsko-ukraińskie 1943-1948, Warszawa 1999, p. 238-241. The most known crimes occurred on 3 March 1945. In the village of Pawłokoma (district Brzozów), in which the company AK soldiers under the command of Lieutenant Józef Biss "Wacław" murdered approx. 360 Ukrainians, see more: E. Misiło, Pawłokoma 3 III 1945, Warszawa 2006.

[27] In the literature there are different numbers of deported to the USSR. According to the data found by E. Misiło there were 483808 people (E. Misiło, Repatriacja czy deportacja..., vol. 2, p. 357). Jan Pisuliński states there were 494,805 people deported (J. Pisuliński, Przesiedlenia ludności ukraińskiej z Polski do USSR w latach 1944-1947, Rzeszów 2009, p. 508). 70 000 Lemkos are mentioned in: R. Reinfuss, Śladami Łemków, Warszawa 1990, p. 129; and Andrzej Kwilecki estimates the numer for about 96800 (A. Kwilecki, Fragmenty najnowszej historii Łemków [ze szczególnym uwzględnieniem Łemków sądeckich], „Rocznik Sądecki", 1967, vol. VIII, p. 82).

[28] K. Urban, Kościół prawosławny w Polsce 1945-1970 (rys historyczny), Kraków 1996, p. 115; G. Kuprianowicz, Prawosławnaja Cerkwa na Chołmszczyzni, Piwdennom Pidliaszi i Lemkowszczini w 40 roki XX st. i akcja „Wisła", „Cerkiewny Wiestnik", 2002, no 3.

[29] A. Kwilecki, Fragmenty najnowszej historii..., p. 276-277; J. Kwiek, Żydzi, Łemkowie, Słowacy w województwie krakowskim w latach 1945-1949/50, Kraków 1998, p. 107.

The final element of dislocation, the resettlement of the remaining population in Lemkovyna, was "Operation Vistula" [*Akcja Wisła*]. The whole resettlement was the result of processes derived from the political guidelines of the Polish communist politicians of the time. The main feature of this resettlement was coercion, as the transferees could not decide their own fate. This was a violation of fundamental human rights. As Krzysztof Skubiszewski stated, "The United Nations Charter, ratified by Poland in 1945, giving, among others, guarantees of freedom from interference in family and home life, and the right to choose one's residence, was affected by the Operation "Vistula" in relation to many Lemko families"[30].

"Operation Vistula" applied methods to the civilian population which were a means to a general goal: to create an ideal state based having political boundaries identical to the boundaries of nationality. The operation was conducted in a specific political and psychological atmosphere. Hatred of strangers (Germans, Jews, Ukrainians) was skillfully fueled by the authorities and was largely accepted by Polish society. In many cases, attitudes toward non-Polish populations were marked by hatred, humiliation of national and human dignity. Note, however, that Lemkos were subjected to a totalitarian system, which was beginning to function in Poland; actions against the Lemko people were part of a system that enslaved the whole of society.

The concept of "Operation Vistula" should not be taken as confined only to the fact of forced resettlement. It has a very broad scope of meaning including, besides the forced relocations, issues related to the organization of resettlement, the activity of various kinds of civilian authorities (State Repatriation Office, Polish State Railways) and military (military courts), and the settlement of the displaced population into new territories. It was also accompanied by administrative and legal procedures aiming at the speedy assimilation of Lemkos, restrictions on their personal freedom, and deprivation of rights to their property left behind in southeastern Poland.

Overall, during the "Operation Vistula" 140,577 people were deported to the so-called Recovered Territories[31]. They were settled in nine prov-

[30] K. Skubiszewski, Akcja „Wisła" a prawo międzynarodowe, "Tygodnik Powszechny", March 1990.

[31] The displaced people took with them, among others, 20460 horses and 45729 cows, AAN, State Repatriation Office (PUR), sygn. XII/119. It is significant to notice

inces in 71 counties[32]. The approximate number of Lemkos should be set at 30-35 thousand people [others say 50,000]. This constituted approximately 20% of the total deported population. The precise number of people settled in the individual districts is very difficult to determine. Often the quantitative data of the displaced varies in the documentation retained in the State Repatriation Office (PUR) and by military authorities[33]. An additional difficulty was so-called "relocations to other counties" or arbitrary relocation of those already resettled. It was planned to further relocate, among others, 119 families from the Głogów district (out of 152 settled there), and 24 families (out of 126 settled) in the Zielona Góra district. Within the limits of the Kożuchów district 22 families were relocated. 166 families were intended to move to other counties. Some people were also relocated from the districts of Gorzów Wielkopolski (27 families) and Skwierzyna (53 families)[34].

The main objective of deportations of Lemkos was maximum dispersion, and then assimilation into a new Polish environment. An example illustrating this process can be Florynka, a village (928 people were resettled), whose inhabitants were dispersed in 6 counties and over 30

the data were collected on 28 August 1947. At the same time it was reported that the collecting transports were still continuing to go. Adding to that several thousand detainees in Jaworzno and prisons, and the action from 1950 we get a larger number of deportees. According to E. Misiło the total number of displaced did not exceed 150 thousand. Akcja „Wisła". Dokumenty, ed. by E. Misiło, Warszawa 1993, p. 33. On the other hand the data collected by A. Maryański seem understated. He specifies the number of displaced approx. 120 thousand, see: A. Maryański, Migracje w świecie, Warszawa 1984, p. 112.

[32] In the Białystok Province 995 people were settled, in Gdańsk Province 5280, in Koszalin Province 31169, in Olsztyn Province 56625, in Opole Province 2542, in Poznań Province 1437, in Szczecin Province 15058, in Wrocław Province 15491, and in Zielona Góra Province 10870, Akcja „Wisła". Dokumenty..., p. 443-448. According to my findings 11768 people from Operation "Vistula" were settled in region of Zielona Góra, see: S. Dudra, Poza małą ojczyzną. Łemkowie na Ziemi Lubuskiej, Wrocław 2008, p. 51.

[33] About the Lemko settlement from the Operation "Vistula" see: A. Kwilecki, Problemy socjologiczne Łemków na Ziemiach Zachodnich, "Kultura i Społeczeństwo", 1966, no 3; idem, Zagadnienia stabilizacji Łemków na Ziemiach Zachodnich, "Przegląd Zachodni", 1966, no 6; K. Pudło, Łemkowie, Proces wrastania w środowisko Dolnego Śląska 1947-1985, Wrocław 1987; S. Dudra, Łemkowie. Deportacja i osadnictwo ludności łemkowskiej na Środkowym Nadodrzu w latach 1947-1960, Głogów 1998.

[34] AAN, Ministry of Recovered Territories (MZO), Inspection Department, sygn. 1032, Distribution and the plan of transfers of the displaced people from the Operation "Vistula" in districts Głogów, Zielona Góra and Kożuchów.

towns. In general, they lived in small groups of one to five families[35]. If it was found that some displaced people were accompanied by "some elements of the intelligentsia, they were ordered to place these elements absolutely separately and away from areas inhabited by them"[36]. In this way they tried to deprive the Lemkos of care from educated people (priests, teachers).

As reference materials collected by Andrzej Kwilecki indicate, residents coming from a single Lemko village usually ended up split across many — a dozen or several dozen — towns or villages across several counties, often far away from each other. The number of districts inhabited by Lemkos in the Polish "Recovered Territories" exceeded by a large factor the number of districts in which they had lived in the Carpathians. In the mountains they lived within two provinces and five counties, but as a result of resettlement they were in five provinces and 65 counties. For example, Lemkos from the district of Sanok were settled across 16 counties, those from Gorlice across 20, and those from Nowy Sącz across 19[37].

Most resettlement took place between April and July 1947, when most of the Lemko population was displaced *en masse*. Families were resettled individually during the period August-October 1947. Resettlements as part of "Operation Vistula" continued in 1948 (among others, those released from the camp in Jaworzno) and had not ended even in January-April 1950, when a dozen families were displaced from the Nowy Targ district communities of Szlachtowa, Jaworki, Biała Woda and Czarna Woda to Szczecin Province. The Director of the Political Department of the Ministry of Public Administration (MAP) justified the expulsions because of alleged cooperation of this population with the Ukrainian Insurgent Army (UPA) troops and important economic interests in the Nowy Targ region[38]. According to Roman Drozd, this was the last transport of the "Operation Vistula" except for one from Chełm in 1952[39].

---

[35] A. Kwilecki, Łemkowie. Zagadnienie migracji i asymilacji, Warszawa 1974, p. 113.
[36] AAN, MZO, sygn. 784, MZO Instructions on the distribution of settlers from the Operation "Vistula" on 10 November 1947.
[37] A. Kwilecki, Łemkowie. Zagadnienie ..., p. 115.
[38] AAN, Ministry of Public Administration (MAP), sygn. 781, The letter of the Provincial Office of Kraków to the Political Department of MAP in Warszawa on November 28 1949, ibidem, The letter of the Provincial Office of Kraków to MAP on 29 April 1950.
[39] R. Drozd, Powojenne wysiedlenia Łemków polskich w latach 1944-1950, [in:] Łemkowie, Bojkowie, Rusini. Historia, współczesność, kultura materialna i duchowa, ed. S. Dudra, B. Halczak, A. Ksenicz, J. Starzyński, Legnica-Zielona Góra 2007, p. 141.

The events of "Operation Vistula" and its consequences have been described in a large body of literature that is nonetheless insufficient to relate the real climate of tragedy among the displaced population. If one wants to know and understand the Lemkos during and after the displacement, one should become familiar with the realm of individual and collective psychology.

Their ethnic cleansing began a new period in Lemkos' history. Due to intentional dispersion, social ties were severed. Social structure and intragroup hierarchy were also broken down. The removal of men, women and children from their family environment, and a lack of acceptance in their new surroundings, strongly impacted the nature of the forcibly displaced population. In addition to poor material conditions, a negative stereotype of the population as "displaced criminals" (a term found in the source materials) developed.[40] This, as well as their recognition of their resettlement as unlawful, determined their attitude to the new post-war political reality. The shock of being forced from their land caused the collapse of faith in fundamental legal and moral norms. Accurately characterizing the operation, Kazimierz Podlaski wrote: "We are responsible as a nation for what happened in the course of the Operation "Vistula". We are responsible for the razing of the habitatation of hundreds of thousands of people, turning their land to desert, dispersing over a hundred thousand into adversity. Not to mention the dead, tortured and debased"[41].

"Operation Vistula" must also be assessed from the point of view of postwar conditions, taking into account the experience of Polish society. The ordeal of war and occupation and a negative attitude towards national minorities contributed to the decisions made by the then decision-makers, and this type of solution gained social approval.

"Operation Vistula" started in 1947 and for many of its participants has been continuing to this day. The passage of time has not been able to erase the tragic events and personal experiences. The head of the Polish

---

[40] This issue is discussed among others by: M. Truchan, Nehatywnyj stereotyp Ukrajincia w polskij literaturi, Monachium-Lwów 1992; M. Kmita, Propaganda antyukraińska i kształtowanie się negatywnego stereotypu Ukraińca w czasach PRL, [in:] Problemy Ukraińców w Polsce po wysiedleńczej akcji „Wisła" 1947 roku, ed. W. Mokry, Kraków 1997; G. Motyka, Obraz Ukraińca w literaturze Polski Ludowej, [in:] Polska-Ukraina spotkanie kultur. Materiały z sesji naukowej, ed. T. Stegner, Gdańsk 1997.
[41] K. Podlaski, Białorusini-Litwini-Ukraińcy, Londyn 1985, p. 100.

Autocephalous Orthodox Church, Metropolitan Sawa, in his speech on 15 June 2002 in Chełm, on the occasion of the ceremony commemorating the 55th anniversary of "Operation Vistula" found that

> ...looking at every historical fact, ["Operation Vistula"] can be analyzed in different contexts: political, sociological, economic, religious. However, you should never forget the human dimension of history— that historical events relate primarily to specific people, affecting their lives, fortunes and futures. Speaking of "Operation Vistula" you can not just forget about the purely human context. Let us remember that it was primarily the tragedy of real people who did not understand why and by which law they were thrown out of their ancestral land, the land on which their ancestors had worked for centuries, where they had left the graves of their loved ones, their family house, their own church, in which they were baptized, where they got married. They were transported hundreds of kilometers away from their home thresholds, to an unknown and often hostile environment. Looking at the event with this very human perspective, we have no doubt as to its moral judgment.[42]

The resettlements of the years 1944-1947 completely changed the character of Lemkovyna. Lemkos were deported mostly to the Soviet Ukraine, and then displaced to the so-called Recovered Territories [within Poland]. According to the assumptions of the state authorities, they were to be subjected to a process of assimilation and polonization, the consequence of which was to become their rapid denationalization. Yet despite the complicated sociopolitical context in which Lemkos had to live, they managed to preserve their own identity. According to National Census data from 2011, 10,531 people declared Lemko nationality (including 5.612 people who declared it as their only nationality, 7,086 as a first nationality, and 3,445 as a second nationality)[43]. Among those declaring, Lemko nationality, about five thousand lived in Lower Silesia Province and about two thousand in Małopolska Province (of which about a thousand and a half declared solely Lemko nationality.)[44]

---

[42] „Cerkiewny Wiestnik", 2002, no 3.
[43] Ludność. Stan i struktura demograficzno-społeczna. Narodowy Spis Powszechny Ludności i Mieszkań 2011. Główny Urząd Statystyczny, p. 91 [12.06.2015].
[44] Raport z wyników w województwie dolnośląskim. Narodowy Spis Powszechny Ludności i Mieszkań 2011. Wrocław: Urząd Statystyczny we Wrocławiu, 2012, p. 62-

***

This publication consists of this introduction and six essays on the history and religion of Lemkos[45]. They present, among others, Lemko symbols of martyrdom (such as St. Maksym Sandowicz, the camp at Thalerhof, and Jaworzno) which significantly influenced the strengthening of their own identity. In this process, an important role was played by Orthodox hierarchy and clergy. The Orthodox Church also fulfilled an important role in activities outside of religion. It was a signpost on the road to the formation of a nation. It was particularly important after World War II (1945-1989), when state policy was not conducive to the development of national and religious minorities. Examples of specific religious conditions include, among others, the matter of erecting a parish in Rozdziele and longtime conflict in Polany. The above-mentioned elements became an important link in the evolution of Lemko national identity. The last essay "Lemkos in the United States of America" was written by Arkadiusz Tyda, researcher into the history of Lemkos in the United States.

63; Raport z wyników w województwie małopolskim. Narodowy Spis Powszechny Ludności i Mieszkań 2011. Kraków: Urząd Statystyczny w Krakowie, 2012, p. 105-107.

[45] Some parts of the study have been published in Polish scientific journals.

CHAPTER ONE

Symbols of martyrdom as a part of the shaping of Lemko identity

In the life of every nation there are people and events (sometimes tragic), which significantly define its identity. For the Lemko community such symbols were and are: the priest St. Maksym Sandowicz (also called Maksym Gorlicki) and the events connected with the concentration/internment camps of Thalerhof and Jaworzno.

Maksym Sandowicz – Lemko priest and martyr

Maksym Sandowicz [pronounced San-do-vich] was born on 31 January 1886 in Zdynia in a Greek Catholic family. After graduating from four-year primary school in Gorlice he went on to secondary school in Jasło, and then in Nowy Sącz. After finishing his fourth year of secondary school, due to his poor performance, he dropped out, and entered a novitiate at the Basilian monastery in Krechów. After a short time, disappointed with his spiritual level, he went to the Pochayiv Lavra [monastery] known for its rich Orthodox traditions, where he became a novice. Then he was sent by Archbishop Anthony (Khrapovitsky) to the seminary in Żytomierz (Zhitomyr) from which he graduated in 1911[46].

After his marriage to Pelagia Grygoruk (the daughter of a Orthodox priest) he was ordained a priest by Archbishop Anthony on 17 November 1911 and he was posted to Lemkovyna, where he joined in missionary activity among the local Greek Catholics. He served in Grab, where the faithful went over to the Orthodox jurisdiction because of a conflict with the local Greek Catholic parish priest. He also celebrated liturgies in Wyszowadka and Długie[47].

---

[46] B. Wójtowicz-Huber, Ojcowie narodu. Duchowieństwo greckokatolickie w ruchu narodowym Rusinów galicyjskich (1867-1918), Warszawa 2008, p. 187-189; J. Charkiewicz, Męczennicy XX wieku. Martyrologia prawosławia w Polsce w biografiach świętych, Warszawa 2004, p. 13-15; Żywot Świętego Maksyma Gorlickiego (Sandowicza), "Almanach Diecezjalny", 2005, vol. 1, p. 97.

[47] J. Charkiewicz, op. cit., p. 16-17.

Father Maksym Sandowicz carried out his ministry in Lemkovyna during a counter offensive against the Russophile movement[48] by the Austrian authorities in Galicia. As an Orthodox priest ordained in Russia he was regarded as an enemy of the authorities in Vienna. For this reason, he was prohibited from pastoral activities (evasion of which became a cause for punishment with fines and arrest). As Bernadette Wójtowicz-Huber stated "Sandowicz was an extraordinary personality. Despite the ban on further activities, due to his charisma, deep faith and good repute, he grew into a symbol for the contemporary Lemko community."[49] His popularity grew also because of his attitude to the local community (among other actions he distributed donations collected during services to the poor.)

In 1912, he was arrested (among others, including priest Ignacy Hudyma) as part of anti-Russophile actions by the Austrian authorities and accused of spying and seeking to detach Galicia from the Austro-Hungarian Empire. As pointed out by Włodzimierz Osadczy, at "the eve of war the show trial of Orthodox agitators was to be a warning to any groups sympathizing with Russia in the country, and not only for the Rus', but also for Polish nationalist democrats who were growing in power"[50]. The trial ended, however, with acquittal and the clergyman left detention on 7 June 1914.

After the outbreak of World War I, Fr. Maksym was re-arrested and on 6 September 1914 he was executed without trial during new repressions of people suspected of pro-Russian sympathies. The execution took place in the courtyard of the Gorlice prison at approximately 6 a.m. It was witnessed by residents of Gorlice and neighboring towns who were in prison on charges of Russophile sympathy, including members of the priest's family[51]. According to reports the clergyman cried at the last

---

[48] Russophile movement was a linguistic and literary and socio-political trend existing among the Ruthenian population in Galicia, Bukowina and Carpathian Rus. It formed from the early nineteenth century. It stated among others national-cultural and state community with the Russian nation. It competed with the Ukrainian national movement, see more: W. Osadczy, Święta Ruś. Rozwój i oddziaływanie idei prawosławia w Galicji, Lublin 2007; B. Wójtowicz-Huber, op. cit.

[49] B. Wójtowicz-Huber, op. cit., p. 188.

[50] W. Osadczy, op. cit., p. 565-567, see also: M. Bołtryk, Sąd nad Świętym Maksymem, Gorlice 2014.

[51] Pelagia Sandowicz was deported from Gorlice to the camp in Thalerhof, where she bore a son, christened after his father with name Maksym. In later years he also became an Orthodox priest.

minute: *Long live holy Orthodoxy! Long live Holy Rus'!*[52]. The funeral of Fr. Sandowicz took place without the participation of the family, in the cemetery in Gorlice. In 1922, at the request of his father and wife, his remains were exhumed and transfered to the cemetery in Zdynia. This was co-sponsored by Lemko immigrants residing in the USA. [His remains now rest in the Orthodox Cathedral in Gorlice].

Thalerhof

The Internment/Concentration camp in Thalerhof [south of Graz in the Stiermark province of Austria proper] was created by the Austro-Hungarian authorities primarily for Rus' (from Galicia and Bukowina) accused of Russophilism; the first arrests took place before hostilities actually began. The main charges were accusations of favoring Russia and of concomitant activities against the [Habsburg] state. With the outbreak of war mass arrests began, most of which were carried out on the basis of lists provided to the authorities by activists of the Ukrainian political movement. Representatives of the Ukrainian party, taking advantage of military concern, placed on the lists mainly representatives of the intelligentsia: doctors, lawyers, priests, as well as political activists, students and politically involved peasants. The arrests took place in the atmosphere of war psychosis caused by early failures in the war with Imperial Russia.

The first groups of prisoners were sent to Thalerhof as early as 4 September 1914. In 1914, virtually the whole Lemko intelligentsia with the Russophile views were arrested by the Austrian authorities (including the priests Teofil Kaczmarczyk, Dymitr Chylak, and Jan Polański; lawyers Jarosław Kaczmarczyk and Teofil Kuryłło; and cultural activists Dymitr Kaczor, Semeon Pyzh, Metody Trochanowski and Dymitr Wysłocki. In one of the first transports there were also Pelagia Sandowicz, widow of Father Maksym, and Father Maksym's father Tymoteusz[53]. Peasants, too, did not avoid arrest. The main reason for arrest was suspicion about possible cooperation with tsarist Russia. Until the winter of 1914/1915 there were no barracks in the camp [built on the southern end of a military

---

[52] J. Charkiewicz, op. cit., p. 20-22. According to another version the priest shouted: Long live the people and holy Russian Orthodox Church, see: Żywot Świętego Maksyma Gorlickiego (Sandowicza), "Almanach Diecezjalny", 2005, vol. 1, p. 101.

[53] A. Rydzanicz, Galicyjska Golgota, "Przegląd Prawosławny", 2004, no 10, p. 8; see more: P. Stefanowski, Łemkowie w Thalerhof ie, "Magury 82", p. 41-48.

airport in village of Thalerhof]. The prisoners slept on the ground in the open air, rain and cold[54].

In the camp (which operated until 10 May 1917) there were approximately seven thousand people (Russians, Ukrainians, Gypsies, Lemkos, Jews and Poles). 1767 imprisoned people died as a result of hunger, bad sanitary conditions and the outbreak of cholera. By 1915 Lemkos from 151 villages were imprisoned in Thalerhof; 168 of them died.[55]

In the interwar period Thalerhof and the story of Father Maksym became important elements in shaping the national consciousness of Lemkos. The solemn celebration of events related to the martyrdom of Lemkos during World War I became the basis of Lemko identity. The martyrdom of the priest Maksym seemed to be the foundation for the growth of Orthodoxy— songs and poems were written in honor of the clergyman, his portraits appeared in the homes, pilgrimages to his grave were organized.[56] [Oddly enough two other Sandowiczes were also killed, of which nothing is heard.]

After World War I a "Cult of Thalerhof " was created and developed in Russophile circles. In this framework, reunions of Thalerhof inmates were organized, special services were celebrated, books and diaries were printed. On the twentieth anniversary of Thalerhof (1934) Jarosław Ropicki wrote *Thalerhofska kantata* (it has been performed during Thalerhof events up till now). Numerous Thalerhof crosses and monuments were established (among others in Bartne), at which Lemko patriotic ceremonies were held. In the message of 7 September 1934 addressed to the Lemkos, on the occasion of the celebrations commemorating the twentieth anniversary of the martyrdom of Fr. Maksym and the memory of those imprisoned and murdered in Thalerhof, Metropolitan Dionizy

---

[54] See: Thalerhof : Eternal Memory!, http://orthodoxengland.org.uk/pdf/Thalerhof .pdf [20.06.2014]; The Story of Thalerhof . We Should Not Forget, http://www. carpatho-rusyn.org/kr/taler.htm [20.06.2015]; Terrorism in Bohemia. Medill Mc-Cormick Gets Details of Austrian Cruelty There, http://query.nytimes.com/mem/ archive-free/pdf [20.06.2014].

[55] Thalerhof : Eternal Memory!, http://orthodoxengland.org.uk/pdf/Thalerhof .pdf [20.06.2014]. The list of names of people who died in Thalerhof was included in the "Almanach Diecezjalny", 2006, vol. 2, p. 214-258. The document was prepared for publication by Father Piotr Pupczyk.

[56] P. Trochanowski, Postać Świętego Maksyma w twórczości literackiej, "Almanach Diecezjalny", 2005, vol. 1, p. 121-138; Wiersze i pieśni o Św. Maksymie Gorlickim, ibidem, p. 140-149.

wrote: "Martyr Maksym Sandowicz's blood, shackles and the sufferings of people in Thalerhof marked the past, a close spiritual renewal and resurrection. And the fact, the resurrection of the people of Lemkovyna occurred. [...] Today's [commemoration] is holy for all Orthodox Lemkovyna — a day of prayer, of memories of your fathers and brothers who gave their lives for the faith and the nation. On this day I am with you, my beloved little children. God bestows eternal rest in a just place for everyone that we remember today [...]. I bless the Council of the Orthodox Spiritual Mission to organize annually in the village Czarne, on the first Sunday of September, a holy remembrance of the martyrs suffering for the faith and the people. Let this day be a day of prayer, of unity of the entire Lemkovyna, a holiday of Orthodoxy, a day of manifestation of the life, wealth and natural beauty of our Christian faith."[57]

In the Lemko Region, memorial obelisks and shrines were erected in honor of the victims[58]. In the churches papers were read, concerts of religious songs were held. These celebrations were of great significance for Lemkos. According to the accounts of 1935 from the village Czarne: "Around 80 processional crosses and banners, a few patriotic and national flags and 29 wreaths decorated with ribbons with occasional inscriptions were gathered [...] One brought out of the church the Lemko standard, on one side of which was the Pochayiv icon of the Mother of God, on the other an eight-pointed cross in a wreath of thorns and an inscription with Father Maksym Sandowicz's last words: "Long live Holy Orthodoxy – Long live Holy Rus' "[59]. In 1935 the "Fr. Maksym Sandowicz Brotherhood of the Orthodox Church" was established in Czarne on the initiative of parish priest Jerzy Pawłyszyn[60]. This trend continued until the outbreak of World War II. The cult of the priest Maksym as a martyr developed

---

[57] Cit. from: R. Dubec, Recepcja św. Maksyma Gorlickiego w Polsce i na świecie, "Almanach Diecezjalny" 2005, Gorlice 2006, vol. 1, p. 107-108.

[58] On 9 September 1934 in Czarne, on the initiative of Fr. Konstanty Hawryłkow, a monument was erected in honor of Fr. Sandowicz and victims of the camp in Thalerhof . Bishop of Ostrog Szymon, delegated by the Metropolitan Dionizy, took part in its unveiling, see: R. Rydzanicz, O przeszłości trzeba mówić, "Przegląd Prawosławny", 2007, no 10, p. 8.

[59] The celebration of the memory of Fr. Maksym Sandowicz and victims of the camp in Thalerhof in the village Czarne in 1935 gathered more than 8 thousand participants from 27 villages, see: A. Barna, Kronika-Litopis żytia religijno-gromadiańskogo parafii seła Czorne na Lemkowyni 1770-1970, Legnica 1997, p. 47-51.

[60] J. Moklak, Łemkowszczyzna w Drugiej Rzeczypospolitej. Zagadnienia polityczne i wyznaniowe, Kraków 1997, p. 98.

in the USA too[61].

In post World War II Poland, the cult of the martyrdom of Maksym Sandowicz played an important role among Orthodox Lemkos. This refers to both the faithful settled after 1947 on the Recovered Territories, as well as those returning to Lemkovyna after 1956. Icons of Maksym Sandowicz began to appear in Lemko churches, despite the fact that his cult was not officially sanctioned by the Orthodox Church (carrying out a canonization in communist Poland was not possible for political reasons)[62]. The memory of the death of the priest was a living element in the religious life of Lemkos (a commemoration of the 70th anniversary of his death was held in Zdynia with Archbishop Adam of Przemyśl and Nowy Sącz presiding.)[63].

The cult of martyrdom of the Lemko cleric led to his *prosłowlenije* (canonization). The celebrations took place on 9-10 September 1994 in Zdynia. It was the first such event in the history of the Polish Autocephalous Orthodox Church. The ceremonies were presided over by the Metropolitan of Warsaw and All Poland Bazyli (Doroszkiewicz)[64].

The priest-martyr Maksym Sandowich is today the symbol of the Lemkos, continuing the traditions and the Orthodox faith of their forefathers. One of the manifestations of this veneration are the icons with his image in many Lemko churches and chapels dedicated to him. Parish feasts on their patron saint's day are celebrated solemnly. St. Maksym unites Orthodox Lemkos both in western Poland as well as in historical Lemkovyna (consecrated in 1992, the cathedral Church of the Holy Trinity in Gorlice is a monument to the martyrdom of Fr. Maksym Sandowicz)[65]. A new Orthodox church under the patronage of the saint was built in Głogów.

The process of commemoration of St. Maksym is ongoing. In 1994

---

[61] See: R. Dubec, Recepcja św. Maksyma Gorlickiego w Polsce i na świecie, "Almanach Diecezjalny", 2005, vol. 1, p. 110-111, 115.
[62] A. Rydzanicz, O przeszłości trzeba rozmawiać..., p. 8-10.
[63] J. Charkiewicz, op. cit., p. 25-27.
[64] In 1996 Russian Church outside Russia also recognized Father Maksym Sandowicz as a saint. In 2001, Synod of the Russian Orthodox Church established a local holiday of the Saint Galician of the Council, which is celebrated in the Diocese of Lwow. Maksym Sandowicz was included in the Council of Saints, see: Żurnał zasiedanija Swiaszczennogo Sinoda od apriela 2001 goda, www.mospat.ru [20.06.2015].
[65] See more: R. Dubec, Recepcja św. Maksyma Gorlickiego w Polsce i na świecie..., p. 103-119.

a plaque was installed on the courthouse in Gorlice with an inscription in the Lemko language with information about his death in that place.[66] In 1997 the Orthodox sports organizations of the Republic of Poland, as well as youth belonging to the Brotherhood of Orthodox Youth of the Diocese of Przemyśl-Nowy Sącz, chose the saint as their patron. On their initiative the "Bicycling Trails of St. Maksym Gorlicki" were organized.[67] In addition, in 2003 a new monument called *Lemko Golgotha* was erected on his grave.[68]

On 28 November 2006 the Council of Bishops of Polish Autocephalous Orthodox Church decided to move the relics of St. Maksym from the municipal cemetery in Zdynia to Holy Trinity Cathedral in Gorlice. The ceremony took place on 5 September 2007.[69] In 2012, the city council of Gorlice, at the request of the Orthodox bishop of Gorlice Paisjusz (Martyniuk), established Maksym Gorlicki as the patron saint of the Orthodox residents of the city[70].

Veneration of the priest-martyr continues to strengthen, and has become an important factor in the religious life of Orthodox Lemkos.

Jaworzno

An important element in the ordeal of displaced Lemkos were events related to the labor camp in Jaworzno[71]. Even before the implementa-

---

[66] J. Charkiewicz, op. cit., p. 25-27.
[67] "Antyfon", 1998, no 1-2, p. 38-42; "Antyfon" 2000, no 1, p. 35.
[68] It was designed by his grandson Michał Sandowicz, see: A. Rydzanicz, Hory płakały wereśniom, "Przegląd Prawosławny", 2007, no 10, p. 4-8.
[69] J. Charkiewicz, op. cit., p. 28-29; A. Rydzanicz, Hory płakały wereśniom..., p. 4.
[70] See: Czworo się wstrzymało, http://www.gorlice24pl [10.12.2013].
[71] The camp in Jaworzno was created in 1943 as one of the many branches of Auschwitz. It was then taken over by the Department of Prisons and Camps of the Ministry of Public Security. Germans, Poles, Ukrainians, as well as ethnically uncertain groups (Silesians)were held there. As Zygmunt Woźniczka stated Jaworzno was both a labor camp, penal camp and POW camp. These functions were intertwined and often were hard to distinguish. It was the largest place of torture leading in terms of the number of dead to other camps and prisons, Z. Woźniczka, Obozy w systemie faszystowskim i stalinowskim (zarys problemu), [in:] Obóz dwóch totalitaryzmów – Jaworzno 1943-1956, ed. R. Terlecki, Jaworzno 2007, vol. 2, p. 45; see also B. Kopka, Obóz w Jaworznie w systemie polskiego Gułagu, [in:] Obóz dwóch totalitaryzmów – Jaworzno 1943-1956..., p. 17 and next; M. Wyrwich, Łagier Jaworzno. Z dziejów czerwonego terroru, Warszawa 1995. Ukrainian sub-camp

tion of "Operation Vistula", on 23 April 1947, the Political Bureau of the Central Committee of The Polish Workers' [communist] Party decided to transform the Central Labor Camp in Jaworzno, in existence since January 1945, into a camp for Ukrainian civilians suspected of favoring the [anti-Polish Ukrainian] underground. As Eugeniusz Misiło stated, the decision was one of three elements of "Operation Vistula", which was to isolate the Ukrainian intelligentsia and all other people with a similar attitude or position in the Ukrainian social hierarchy who did not give a guarantee of submission to the expulsions[72].

Its location was a relatively small distance from the Auschwitz (Oświęcim) railroad station, the main distribution point for the population that had been displaced as part of the "Operation Vistula"[73]. In Auschwitz commanders of the transports opened sealed envelopes [which they received with each new incoming transport] with the encrypted names of destination stations, and then the inhabitants of each village were separated and sent to different parts of Poland. Again, personal details were verified and people "suspected" of cooperating with the UPA [the Ukrainian Insurgent Army] were arrested. The arrests affected the sparse intelligentsia (clergy, teachers, doctors), as well as leftists and former soldiers of the Red Army. However, the primary group of detainees were peasants[74]. An ex-prisoner's report shows that people often ended up in the camp on the basis of imaginary accusations. For example, an interrogator claimed hidden weapons were found in a deportee's house after his deportation.[75]

The main objective of the creation of the "Ukrainian sub-camp" at Jaworzno was the incarceration of activists of the Ukrainian nationalist armed underground or persons suspected of such activities. However, as Igor Hałagida stated, except for some difficult-to-estimate number of actual members or associates of some Ukrainian conspiracy, behind the

---

was liquidated in January 1949, and its last inmates were transferred to Kraków and then to the prison in Grudziądz. A prison for juveniles was located originally in Jaworzno (1949-1955), and then Jaworzno Central Prison functioned to its close in 1956.

[72] E. Misiło, Jak PRL rozwiązywała kwestię ukraińską, "Tygodnik Powszechny", March 1990.

[73] K. Miroszewski, Ukraińcy i Łemkowie w Centralnym Obozie Pracy Jaworzno, [in:] Pamiętny rok 1947, ed. M. E. Ożóg, Rzeszów 2001, p. 212.

[74] Ibidem.

[75] Unauthorized report by Mikołaj P., the prisoner of Jaworzno, from village Biernatów (district Szprotawa) on 15 June 1990 (private author's archives).

barbed wire of the camp there were mostly persons without any connection with the underground. Sometimes their presence was completely
accidental, and their only fault was often the fact that they were Ukrainians[76]. According to calculations by E. Misiło not fewer than 3873 people
altogether were imprisoned in the "Ukrainian sub-camp", including more
than 800 women and several children. In the camp at least 24 children
were born, of which an unspecified number died as a result of, among
other reasons, the prevailing starvation and diseases.[77] In the final phase
of "Operation Vistula", approximately 156 people who had returned to
their original homes were sent to the camp.[78] As a result of malnutrition,
brutal interrogation and torture 162 people died.

In February 1948 the communist authorities started releasing prisoners. By March 1948 approximately three thousand imprisoned people
had been released. The last group to be released was the clergy, who, in
early January 1949, were taken to the prison in Montelupich in Cracow,
and then to the criminal-investigation prison in Grudziądz[79].

It is difficult to determine the number of Orthodox imprisoned in
Jaworzno. Among them there were both people closely associated with the
life of the Church (such Józef Bobrowicz, the psalmist at Hrubieszów), as
well as parishioners from most pastoral centers (including 27 people from
the parish of Bartne, the most from any parish in Lemkovyna, including the Greek Catholic ones). Among the prisoners there were also five
Orthodox clergy[80]. In July 1947 the priests Bazyli Laszenko and Damian

---

[76] Duchowni greckokatoliccy i prawosławni w Centralnym Obozie pracy w Jaworznie
(1947-1949). Dokumenty i materiały, collected and developer by I. Hałagida,
Warszawa 2012, p. 13; about the conditions in the camp see: Jaworzno. Spohady
wjazniw polśkoho koncentracijnoho taboru, ed. B. Huk, M. Iwanyk, Peremyszl-
Toronto-Lwiw 2007.

[77] Archives of the Institute of National Remeberance (AIPN) BU 02482/31, Infor-
mation regarding the imprisonment of Ukrainian civilians in the Central Labour
Camp in Jaworzno in the years 1947-1949 (prepared by E. Misiło, July 1990). As K.
Mieroszewski stated, from each shipment passing through Oświęcim from a few
to a dozen people were left in the camp, which in total accounted for approx. 10%
of all prisoners of the Ukrainian camp. He estimates the number of incarcerated
Ukrainians and Lemkos to 3761 people, see: K. Miroszewski, Ukraińcy i Łemkowie w
Centralnym Obozie Pracy Jaworzno, [in:] Pamiętny rok 1947..., p. 212.

[78] E. Misiło, Ukraińcy w obozie koncentracyjnym w Jaworznie 1947-1949, [in:] Historia
martyrologii więźniów obozów odosobnienia w Jaworznie 1939-1956, ed. K. Miroszewski i Z. Woźniczka, Jaworzno 2002, p. 69.

[79] Duchowni greckokatoliccy i prawosławni w Centralnym Obozie Pracy w Jaworznie...,
p. 33.

[80] 22 Greek Catholic priests were also imprisoned in The Central Labor Camp in

Towstiuk were detained. The latter, according to Eugenia Iwanyk's recollections, was taken by "the military straight out of the church. A rifle was hung around his neck instead of a cross, and he was led around Waręż, to derision: "Here is a Banderite priest."[81] In August, other Orthodox priests were arrested: Mikołaj Kostyszyn, Józef Kundeus and Aleksy Nestorowicz. They were arrested after resettlement by the officers of the Provincial Public Security Office in Olsztyn. As pointed out by Igor Hałagida, except for one Greek Catholic clergyman, none of the priests was imprisoned under a court order; no prosecutor's sanction had been issued to arrest any of them[82].

Already on 8 July 1947 Fr. Aleksy Baranow, the Lublin district Dean informed the church authorities in Warsaw about the arrest of the priests D. Towstiuk and B. Laszenko[83]. A few days later the Warsaw Orthodox Spiritual Consistory (WDKP) attempted to provide assistance, as well as requesting the reasons for the arrest of and the possible release of the Orthodox clergy. From July 1947 to March 1948 WDKP contacted the Ministry of Recovered Territories, the Ministry of Public Administration, Ministry of Public Security and the Military Prosecutor's Office in Cracow regardings this case.[84] Moreover, in September 1947 Fr. Aleksander Surwiłło, the Orthodox parish priest in Cracow (he also served as Dean

---

Jaworzno.

[81] Cit. from: Duchowni greckokatoliccy i prawosławni w Centralnym Obozie pracy w Jaworznie..., p. 35. It is Worth noticing Fr. D. Towstiuk was born in vilage Mamaji-wce near Czerniowiec (then Habsburg monarchy) and till 1954 he had Romanian citizenship. In 1951 despite the efforts he did not manage to acquire the confirmation of the citizenship in Romanian embassy. Till his departure to Poland in 1957 he was a stateless person.

[82] Formal regulation of this matter took place only in 1949, see: Duchowni grecko-katoliccy i prawosławni w Centralnym Obozie pracy w Jaworznie..., p. 33.

[83] K. Urban, Prześladowanie duchowieństwa prawosławnego w Polsce po 1945 roku (przyczynek do losu uwiezionych w Centralnym Obozie Pracy w Jaworznie), "Cerkiewny Wiestnik", 1992, no 4, p. 32.

[84] The source documents are cited by Kazimierz Urban and Igor Hałagida. WDKP letter to the Ministry of Public Administration of the Orthodox clergy arrested of 19 July 1947 and WDKP letter to the Ministry of Recovered Territories of 11 August 1947 on the arrest of Fathers Aleksy Nestorowicz, Mikołaj Kostyszyn and Józef Kundeus. Moreover, WDKP wrote a letter to the Ministry of Public Security about the case of the arrested clergy (mentioned priests: A. Nesterowicz and M. Kostyszyn). They stated that "Consistory do not suppose the clergy have committed any reprehensible acts and thinks their arrest was due to misunderstanding", AIPN, Ministry of Public Security (MBP), 0296/18, vol. 1, A letter of WDKP to Office of Public Security in Olsztyn on 12 August 1947; K. Urban, Prześladowanie duchowieństwa..., doc. 3 and 4, p. 33-34.

of the Cracow area) was authorized to explain the reasons for detention of the Orthodox clergy, and to assist them[85] (although his actions in this matter are not known). The Church authorities were informed about the arrests of the clergy only by the Ministry of Recovered Territories, and not until November 1947. They also sought explanations for the arrests from the Ministry of Public Security[86]. Despite further actions they did not receive any response to these letters.

The conditions in which the prisoners lived were lacking any precepts of hygiene (no soap or toilet paper). Nutritional status was also deplorable. According to the memoirs of former prisoner meals were prepared in insufficient quantity and of very poor quality. They also lacked drinking water[87]. A displaced person from the village of Bieliczna in Gorlice County, recalls his stay in the camp: "the conditions there were similar to those in a concentration camp: being awakened at night, interrogations and hard labor, and above all lack of food. The authorities put those imprisoned through so much, that to this day victims are afraid of talking about it. Only tears appear in their eyes."[88]

The fate of the prisoners in Jaworzno is known from extensive literature. The wardens used various kinds of harassment against the clergy, who were forced to do exhausting physical labor, publicly humiliated, and prevented from performing religious services.[89] They were also accused of belonging and supporting the Ukrainian underground (e.g., Fr. Damian Towstiuk). Their arrest dramatically affected the fate of the families they left behind. Fr. Towstiuk's pregnant wife and his son were resettled in Prabuty (Susz County) as part of "Operation Vistula". The priests Aleksy Nestorowicz and Józef Kundeus's wives were left destitute. [90] They received partial support, among others, from the Committee for

[85] WDKP letter to Fr. A. Surwiłło of 24 September 1947, see: K. Urban, Prześladowania duchowieństwa…, doc. 11, p. 37.

[86] Letter of Ministry of Recovered Territories to WDKP of 15 November 1947, K. Urban, Prześladowania duchowieństwa…, doc. 12, p. 38.

[87] Unauthorized report by Mikołaj P. from village Biernatów – Szprotawa district (private author's archives).

[88] Unauthorized report by Józef W., an inhabitant of village Bieliczna (private author's archives).

[89] About living conditions in The Central Labor Camp in Jaworzno see: K. Miroszewski, Ukraińcy i Łemkowie w Centralnym Obozie Pracy Jaworzno, [in:] Pamiętny rok 1947…, p. 215-219.

[90] Aleksandra Nestorowicz in her letter to WDKP wrote: „[...] Please help me, also my husband, because we are about to die of hunger and cold. Please take into consideration what costs me my husband, I have sold the rest of my things and I'm

Aid to the Displaced People in the Recovered Territories.[91]

As aforementioned, releases from the camp in Jaworzno began in February 1948 but priests were detained longest. Finally, the Orthodox priests M. Kostyszyn, J. Kundeus, B. Laszenko, and A. Nestorowicz were released from the camp on 12 December 1948[92]. According to a report, all received release orders and "made a commitment of confidentiality as to the circumstances of their interrogation."[93]

The isolation of the Lemko intellectual elite in Jaworzno was to deprive the rest of the Lemkos of their "guides" and thus break them down into a crude ethnic mass susceptible to polonization. Myrosław Truchan stresses that Jaworzno became as much a symbol of the suffering of the population as Thalerhof and Bereza Kartuska [a camp used by the Polish government to intern undesireables in the 1930s] [94].

***

The figure of St. Maksym Sandowicz and events related to the camps in Thalerhof and Jaworzno are important elements in the history of Lemkos. They also became the symbols of shaping their national identity. Today, they are also an important part of strengthening the Orthodox faith.

---

helping my husband", Letter of Aleksandra Nestorowicz to WDKP of February 1948, K. Urban, Prześladowania duchowieństwa…, doc. 16, p. 39. See also: The letter of Lubov Kundeus to the Military Prosecutor's Office in Kraków from 29th October 1948, [in:] Duchowni greckokatoliccy i prawosławni w Centralnym Obozie pracy w Jaworznie…, p. 178.

[91] The Committee was established on 24 July 1947 by Metropolitan Dionizy. Its task was to determine the place of residence of the displaced Orthodox population, organizing material assistance and pastoral care for them, see: K. Urban, Ks. Stefan Biegun (1903-1983). Zapis jednego życia, Kraków 2000, p. 102.

[92] At the same time 13 Greek Catholic priests were released as well.

[93] Duchowni greckokatoliccy i prawosławni w Centralnym Obozie pracy w Jaworznie…, p. 195. Local security authorities continued their supervision. They were subjected to constant supervision (they were monitored their activities in parishes, checked the contents of their sermons, contacts with the faithful and people outside the parish were checked, their correspondence was censored, were often called in for interrogation).

[94] M. Truchan, Ukrajinci w Polszczi pislia druhoji switowoji wijny 1944-1984, Nowy York 1990, p. 59.

Rus' Church in Nizny Komarnyk, Slovak side of the border

CHAPTER 2

Hierarchy, clergy, and Orthodox Lemko religious life, 1918-1947

The Orthodox Church played an important role in the history of Lemkovyna. To the end of the seventeenth century Lemkovyna was part of the Orthodox Diocese of Przemyśl[95]. The Greek Catholic Church in this area came into existence only after the accession of the bishop of Przemyśl, Innocenty Winnicki, to the Union of Brest in 1691.[96] It was a reluctant accession because most Lemkos were tied to their faith. The Greek Catholic hierarchy, considering the conservatism of the Lemkos, initially did not introduce any changes in the liturgy or the interior of the church. As a consequence, this allowed the Lemko community to maintain its traditional religious characteristics[97].

As a result of the spread of the provisions of the Union of Brest, Lemkos became, often against their will, members of the Greek Catholic Church. The exact dates of the accession of every parish to the union are not fully known. In the period before the partitions of Poland there were five deaneries of the Uniate church (Biecz, Dukla, Jasło, Krosno, Muszyna) in Lemkovyna. By the mid-eighteenth century, there were Greek Catholic churches in most Lemko villages, comprising a network of 139 parish churches.[98]

[95] Leading pastoral work Orthodox parish in the seventeenth century were part of deaneries: Biecz, Dukla, Jasło, Krosno, Muszyna and Sanok, see: T. A. Olszański, Z dziejów Kościoła na Łemkowszczyźnie, "Chrześcijanin w Świecie", no 179-180, Warszawa 1988, p. 240; more about the Przemyśl Diocese see: M. Bendza, Prawosławna diecezja przemyska w latach 1596-1681. Studium historyczno-kanon-iczne, Warszawa 1982; P. Gerent, Zarys dziejów prawosławnej diecezji przemyskiej, "Almanach Diecezjalny", 2005, vol. 1, Gorlice 2005, p. 21-47.

[96] See: A. Krochmal, Stosunki między grekokatolikami i prawosławnymi na Łemkowszczyźnie w latach 1926-1939, [in:] Łemkowie w historii i kulturze Karpat..., p. 286; J. J. Burski, A. Nowak, Wyznaniowe wczoraj i dziś Łemkowszczyzny, "Rocznik Ruskiej Bursy", 2005, ed. H. Duć-Fajfer, B. Gambal, Gorlice 2005, p. 73.

[97] E. Michna, Łemkowie. Grupa etniczna czy naród, Kraków 1995, p. 54. Only later one began to introduce new elements in the interior of the church (including benches for the faithful, side altars, pulpit).

[98] Z. Budzyński, Struktura terytorialna i stan wiernych Kościoła unickiego na Łemkowszczyźnie w XVIII wieku, [in:] Łemkowie w historii i kulturze Karpat..., p.

At the end of the nineteenth century, as a result of growing process identification of the Greek Catholic faith with the Ukrainian national movement, two non-Ukrainian orientations turned up in Lemkovyna: the Old Rus' (which considered Eastern Slavs members of one great Rus' nation [broadly defined]) and the Russophile ([more narrowly] pro-Imperial Russia). Basically, these two groups treated the "Ukrainian national ideology as a manifestation of unhealthy separatism"[99].

The Lemko process of returning to Orthodoxy started in the early years of the twentieth century. Among others, the strong influence of the Russian Orthodox Church and the Pochayiv Lavra [monastery] affected this.[100] Cases of conversion [changing from a Greek Catholic jurisdiction to an Orthodox jurisdiction] took place before the First World War. In 1911, part of the village of Grab along with the priest Maksym Sandowicz turned to Orthodoxy. Attempts to change jurisdiction were also recorded in other villages.[101] The reasons for changes were, among others, strong pro-Ukrainian agitation, led by some Greek Catholic clergy. Lemkos rejecting this orientation often declared themselves simultaneously as followers of Orthodoxy. This issue became important later on. However, even before the war the situation became so serious that in 1912 the Greek Catholic bishop of Przemyśl Konstanty Czechowicz was informed that in the case "of the arrival of a Ukrainian priest, the whole village goes over to Orthodoxy; the best evidence of this is Grab, where the *pop* [Orthodox priest] has hundreds of parishioners."[102]

273-274.

[99] J. J. Burski, A. Nowak, op. cit., p. 7.

[100] The Holy Dormition Pochayiv Lavra, monastery in Wołyń (Ukraine), its origins date back to the twelfth century. Since the end of the nineteenth century one of its tasks was to conduct missions among Galician Greek Catholics. They also began training future missionaries from Galicia in the pro-Russian and pro-Orthodox spirit. In the interwar period it was the most important monastery of the Polish Autocephalous Orthodox Church. Currently under the jurisdiction of the Ukrainian Orthodox Church Moscow Patriarchate, see: R. Ergetowski, Poczajowska Ławra, "Wrocławskie Studia Wschodnie", 2005, no 9; U. A. Pawluczuk, Życie monastyczne w II Rzeczypospolitej, Białystok 2007; W. Rożko, Peczerni monastyri Wołyni i Polissia, Łuck 2008.

[101] At the turn of 1911/1912 most of the villagers of Czarne, Długie, Lipno, Nieznajowa and Radocyna reported changing religion to Orthodoxy. As a result of repression by the Austrian authorities in most cases there were no conversion to Orthodoxy, see: J. Moklak, Łemkowszczyzna Łemkowszczyzna w Drugiej Rzeczpospolitej. Zagadnienia polityczne i wyznaniowe, Kraków 1997, p. 28-31.

[102] The case reffered to community Świątkowa, cit. after A. Krochmal, op. cit., p. 287.

The period of World War I sharpened a dispute between the Greek Catholics and the minority Orthodox population. This movement was strengthened, among other ways, by the internment of Lemkos with Old Rus' and Russophile orientation in the camp at Thalerhof. They became increasingly in favor of returning to Orthodoxy, as an opportunity for them to preserve their own identity and at the same time to stand up to increasing Ukrainization. A strong echo in Lemkovyna was made by the shooting of Fr. Maksym Sandowicz, accused of favoring Russophilism and Russia, by the Austrian authorities in September 1914. As already mentioned, the repression and persecutions of the First World War and memories of Thalerhof became a permanent focal point of the Lemko community. They also became a factor bonding it with the Orthodox Church.

The revival of the Orthodox religious life of Lemkos started at the beginning of the twentieth century. It was an important element in shaping the identity of the process of this population. In the interwar period it received the support of the Orthodox hierarchy and clergy. It was also eagerly accepted by the population because a substantial part of the Lemkos rejected Ukrainian national consciousness. The attitude of state authorities to it was influenced, in part, by the fact that "Orthodoxy came to Lemkovyna (just as Subcarpathian Rus' in Czechoslovakia) in close connection with Russophilisim"[103]. In January 1921, the Orthodox Metropolitan Jerzy (Jaroszewski) appointed Fr. Wiktor Kozłowski the administrator of an Orthodox parish in Lwów. Due to opposition from the authorities the parish was not established until June 1924; Hieromonk Pantelejmon Rudyk was appointed the parish priest. Beginning in 1926 it served as the deanery for Lemko parishes returning to Orthodoxy.[104]

There were several reasons for the return to Orthodoxy. The main ones included exclusion of the word *pravoslavny* ("Orthodox") from the liturgy by many Greek Catholic priests (often replaced by the word *pravoverny*, "right-believing"); disputes between the faithful and Greek Catholic clergy, including some clergy's disregard of the Lemko language

[103] Cit. by I. Hwat, Istorja Piwnicznoji Łemkiwszczyny do wygnanja Łemkiw, [in:] Łemkiwszczyna, ed. B. Struminski, vol. 1, New York-Paris-Sydney-Toronto 1988, p. 187.

[104] J. Moklak, Kształtowanie się struktury Kościoła prawosławnego na Łemkowszczyźnie w Drugiej Rzeczypospolitej, "Magury 97", p. 14; R. Dubec, Proces odradzania się Kościoła prawosławnego na Łemkowszczyźnie w okresie międzywojennym, "Almanach Diecezjalny 2006", vol. 2, Gorlice 2006, p. 52.

and Lemko customs as well as material issues related to the increase of fees for religious services such as baptisms, weddings, and funerals. In principle, the waves of conversions were affected by the complex socio-political and religious situation in Lemkovyna.

The process of returning to "the faith of the fathers" started on 16 November 1926 with the conversion of the faithful from the village Tylawa (the so-called Schism of Tylawa)[105]. More Lemko mass returns to Orthodoxy took place during the following years through 1932. Most of the villagers of Banica, Bartne, Binczarowa, Czarne, Florynka, Tylawa and Uście Ruskie, among others, returned to Orthodoxy. Entire villages, sometimes along with the Greek Catholic priest (e.g., Izby with Fr. Dymitr Chylak) transferred to Orthodoxy. At the beginning of the 1930s conversions significantly slowed, then after about 1933 stopped.[106] But by then a total of 17,577 Orthodox Lemkos were recorded, whereas in 1921 the number had been estimated at only about 100 people.[107] According to various data conversions took place in 40 to 47 villages[108].

---

[105] According to data from the state authorities 630 out of 703 inhabitants of Tylawa reported a return to Orthodoxy, AAN, The Ministry of Religious Affairs and Public Education (MWRiOP), sygn. 987, Orthodox movement in the Małopolska region, a note of 4 March 1929.

[106] More see: A. Krochmal, Stosunki między grekokatolikami i prawosławnymi na Łemkowszczyźnie w latach 1926-1939, [in:] Łemkowie w historii i kulturze Karpat…, p. 285-297. The period of mass return to Orthodoxy ended with creating in 1934 the Apostolic Administration of Lemkovyna (AAL), whose main aim was to stop the process. The initiators of its establishment were, among others, representatives of the Greek Catholic intelligentsia and clergy with Old Rus orientation, who intended in this way to stop the spread of the Orthodox Church (in fact conversions generally disappeared in this period). The aim was to cut off Lemkos of massive Ukrainian propaganda flowing from political and church the centers of Przemyśl and Lwów. It consisted of nine deaneries separated from the Greek Catholic Diocese of Przemyśl. On their territory there were 121 parishes that were serviced by 130 priests. The number of believers was estimated at 138,045 people. They were subordinated directly to the Holy; more about AAL see: B. Prach, Apostolska Administracja Łemkowszczyzny, [in:] Łemkowie w historii i kulturze Karpat…, p. 299-311; M. Ryńca, Administracja Apostolska Łemkowszczyzny w latach 1945-1947, Kraków 2003; R. Dubec, Powrót Łemków do prawosławia w odrodzonej Rzeczypospolitej Polskiej (1926-1939), part 2, Apostolska Administracja Łemkowszczyzny jako próba zahamowania konwersji „Cerkiewny Wiestnik", 2006, no 2, p. 34-44.

[107] S. Stępień, Życie religijne społeczności ukraińskiej w Drugiej Rzeczypospolitej, [in:] Polska-Ukraina 1000 lat sąsiedztwa, vol. 1, Przemyśl 1990, p. 216.

[108] Lemko population, who returned to Orthodoxy during this period is estimated at more than 20 thousand. According to the data of the Apostolic Administration of Lemkovyna it amounted to 18 thousand. Warsaw metropolis faithful estimated at approx. 25 thousand, see: A. Krochmal, Stosunki między grekokatolikami i

The process of returning to Orthodoxy performed at the turn of the 20s and 30s of the twentieth century fundamentally changed the religious structure of Lemkovyna. In Banica, Bartne, Binczarowa, Czarne, Florynka, Izby, Lipowiec, Świątkowa Wielka, Tylawa and Uście Ruskie the Orthodox constituted the majority of believers.

These events led to the need to create a network of parishes and buildings to fulfill the religious needs of the faithful. In that regard, Metropolitan Dionizy (Waledyński) appealed to all priests coming from Galicia and working in Wołyń to return to their homeland "to their own people, becoming doctors of their souls."[109] In a letter to the state authorities the hierarch stressed that the returns had a "completely natural and spontaneous character, not inspired by any special agitation". And further the movement's "taking wider and wider dimensions absolutely requires settlement and care on the part of church authorities."[110]

The issue of establishing Orthodox parishes in Lemkovyna and the future of this region were the subject of the Orthodox synod convened by Metropolitan Dionizy on 31 October 1927. During its course, decisions were made about the need for legal regulations to create institutions by giving them the status of a parish. It was also decided that the delegated priests should be entitled to the rights of registars and catechists [i.e., they should be recognized by the Polish state and given state stipends][111]. The synod also decided to erect nine Orthodox parishes and to appointment of Fr. Michał Iwaśkow to the position of dean [head of a group of parishes].[112] It is also worth mentioning that the hierarch personally supported financially the construction of some Orthodox churches (among others, in Lipna)[113].

However, legal recognition of the Orthodox parishes formed in Lemkovyna by authorities was significantly drawn out. The first legalization

---

prawosławnymi na Łemkowszczyźnie w latach 1926-1939, [in:] Łemkowie w historii i kulturze Karpat..., p. 290; also J. Moklak, Kształtowanie się struktury Kościoła prawosławnego na Łemkowszczyźnie w Drugiej Rzeczypospolitej, "Magury 97", Warszawa 1997.

[109] Cit. by R. Dubec, Proces odradzania się Kościoła prawosławnego..., p. 57. Metropolitan Dionizy, among others, delegated to Lemkovyna priests M. Hrycaj, S. Łazuka, M. Popiel, M. Semeniuk, P. Szwajko and O. Wołoszyński.

[110] Cit. by R. Dubec, Proces odradzania się Kościoła prawosławnego..., p. 57.

[111] AAN, MWRiOP, sygn. 1043, The minutes of the meeting of the Synod of the Orthodox Church of October 31 1927.

[112] Ibidem.

[113] See: "Słowo", no 21 of 15 March 1934.

of Orthodox centers as a result of Metropolitan Dionizy's measures took place only in March and April 1928[114]. Lemko returns to Orthodoxy were hampered both by the Greek Catholic priests and partly by local administrative authorities. In those cases, Metropolitan Dionizy intervened repeatedly with the Ministry of Religious Affairs and Public Enlightenment[115]. He appealed, among others, for regulating the religious education of children (in many places where the population had returned to the Orthodox Church, school authorities did not allow Orthodox priests to teach religion) or the handling of metrical books (they were not handed over by the Greek Catholic clergy.)[116] [These books registering birth, marriage and deaths were handled by clergy acting as state functionaries.]

At the end of the 20s the "Orthodox Ecclesiastical Mission" in Lemkovyna was established in Czarne. It was led by Fr. Jerzy Pawłyszyn. Its job was mainly to coordinate pastoral activities and to do cultural and educational work among Lemkos. In order to further support the Orthodox Church in Lemkovyna, Metropolitan Dionizy wrote in his archpastoral letter of 15 May 1931: "The burdens and trials of the young reviving Orthodox community in Lemkivshchyna is in our breast and our Archpastoral eye watches, at every step, your religious life and courageous advocacy for the Orthodox Faith, beloved children in Christ. Your needs are known to us. We know your sorrows as well. Our souls are with you."[117] The hierarch also issued a proclamation addressed to the clergy. He appealed for the establishment of a "Missionary Society", composed of Orthodox priests from the districts of Jasło, Gorlice, Grybów, Nowy Sącz, Krosno and Sanok. In a special order the Metropolitan noted that "missionary meetings are to be held at least three times a year and they aim, besides religious matters, to first and foremost maintain believers in the Orthodox religion"[118]. Fr. Antoni Krynicki was appointed as the organizer

[114] J. Moklak, Łemkowszczyzna w drugiej Rzeczypospolitej. Zagadnienia polityczne i wyznaniowe..., p. 90. The authorities agreed to legalize 6 full-time Orthodox branches: Czarne, Desznica, Mszana, Radocyna, Tylawa (subordinated to the parish in Lwów) and Bogusza (subordinated to the parish in Piotrków).

[115] AAN, MWRiOP, sygn. 987, Metropolitan Dionizy's letter to The Ministry of Religious Affairs and Public Education on the return to Orthodoxy of families from the village Wyszowatka (district Jasło) of 8 June 1928.

[116] Ibidem, Metropolitan Dionizy's letter to The Ministry of Religious Affairs and Public Education of 18 November 1928.

[117] Archives of Orthodox Metropolitan of Warsaw (AWMP), Metropolitan Dionizy's archpastoral letter to the faithful of Lemkovyna of 15 May 1931.

[118] AAN, Ministry of Religious Affairs and Public Education, sygn. 987, The letter of the Provincial Office of Kraków to MWRiOP of 30 November 1931.

and also the first president of "The Missionary Society". Fr. Dymitr Chylak from Izby and the priest-monk Fr. Pantalejmon Rudyk from Tylawa were appointed to the board. "The Mission Council" was established in order to implement the whole project. It consisted of Orthodox priests performing pastoral ministry in Lemkovyna (including Fr. Aleksander Iwanowicz from Bogusza, Fr. Piotr Taranowski from Florynka). It was to develop, based on earlier Metropolitan Dionizy's order, a program for the mission, with the appointment of the places and dates for holding meetings with the faithful.[119]

The first convention of the "Missionary Society" was held on 26 May 1931 in Świątkowa Wielka. A special program designed to encourage the faithful to return to Orthodoxy was prepared. It was also decided to organize further missionary conventions of Orthodox clergy from the area of Lemkovyna (among others, such a convention was held in Florynka on 21 October)[120].

In order to develop cthe ultural and educational life of Lemkos, Orthodox brotherhoods were established, including in Florynka (1930), Bartne (1933) and Czarne (1935). Meetings of delegates of villages returning to Orthodoxy were also organized (both clergy and lay activists participated in them.)

In 1938, a branch of the Pochayiv Lavra was erected in Bartne. Parishioners donated four acres of land to the monastery. It was to affect the entire area of Lemkovyna, spiritually and culturally. The outbreak of war contributed to the suspension (in 1942) of the activities of the monastic center. However, the resident monks left behind a number of melodies from Pochayiv and Wołyń; for many years they were sung by the older generation of parishioners in the church in Bartne.[121]

Throughout the interwar period the Orthodox authorities supported the revival of Orthodoxy in Lemkovyna. Numerous pilgrimages were organized to contribute to the consolidation of the faith. Among other things, in 1932 pilgrimages went from Bogusza to Ľutina (Slovakia) to the holy ceremony *Uspienija Bożej Matery*. Pilgrimages to Vladimirova near Svidnik and to Pochaiv were also organized[122].

---

[119] Ibidem.
[120] Ibidem.
[121] R. Dubec, Z dziejów parafii prawosławnych..., p. 20, 32.
[122] See the wide report: "Słowo", 1932, no 39; R. Dubec, Pokrowytelka Łemkiw, "Antyfon", 2000, no 3.

In the interwar period Orthodoxy in Lemkovyna gained a strong position. The contrast between Old Rus' traditions and an intensifying trend toward Latinization in the Greek Catholic Church was the basis for the return of its inhabitants to "the faith of the fathers". Conversions to Orthodoxy "reflected attempts to find a religious Lemko identity, as close as possible to their local tradition."[123]

The outbreak of World War II fundamentally changed the position of the Orthodox Church. Occupation of parts of Polish territory by the Germans and the Soviet Union changed the organizational structure of the Church. Orthodox parishes on the territories annexed by the Soviet Union were subordinated to the Moscow Patriarchate[124], those in areas connected to the Third Reich to the Archbishop of Berlin Serafin (Karl Lade).[125] An autocephalous Orthodox Church in the General Government was created in 1940. On 30 September 1940 the first meeting of the Council of Bishops was held with the participation of Metropolitan Dionizy and Bishop Tymoteusz (Szretter). On the basis of its resolutions a new administrative division of the church was made. It consisted of three dioceses: Warsaw-Radom, Chełm-Podlasie and Kraków-Lemko.[126] Igumen Palladiusz (Wydybida-Rudenko) was consecrated bishop of the latter on 8 February 1941. On 6 August 1941 the diocese was enlarged by addition of the District of Galicia and adopted the name of Kraków-Lemko-Lwów.[127]

---

[123] R. Dubec, Powrót Łemków do prawosławia..., p. 51.

[124] As stated by M.W. Szkarowskij most Orthodox churches (over 1500) and approx. 3.9 million faithful came under Soviet occupation, M. W. Szkarowskij, Nacistkaja Germania i Prawosławnaja Cerkow (Nacistkaja politika w odnoszenii Prawosławnoj Cerkwi i religioznoje wozrożdennie na okupowannoi teritorii CCCP), Moskwa 2002, p. 113, see more: I. Własowśkyj, Narys istorii Ukraińskoj Prawosławnoji Cerkwy, vol. IV, part 2, New York 1993.

[125] The parishes were in: Bydgoszcz, Gdańsk, Kalisz, Łódź, Poznań, Toruń, Piotrków Trybunalski, Płock, Szczecin and Wrocław, K. Urban, Kościół prawosławny w Polsce 1945-1970, Kraków 1996, p. 150-151.

[126] The Synod of Bishops, chaired by Metropolitan Dionizy held authority over the Autocephalous Orthodox Church in the General Government. Its members were Bishop Hilarion (deputy chairman) and Bishop Palladiusz (secretary). Bishop Tymoteusz was not the member of the Synod because of his Polonophile views, AAN, Ministry of Public Administration (MAP), sygn. 1042, The letter of the director of Religious Department of Ministry of Public Administration Jarosław Demiańczuk to the Minister of Public Administration of 22 June 1945.

[127] The Lemko third deanery was formed in April 1943. In 1944 the diocese became an archbishopric. In 1945-1947, the parishes at Lemkovyna administratively were subject to deanery in Kraków (since the beginning of 1945 the division into

Measures essential to maintain the ownership of the Orthodox Church and securing the necessary religious services were undertaken by church authorities and clergy during the war and occupation. Individual parish houses became meeting places for the faithful, at which decisions were made regarding the vital needs of the parishioners. To a limited extent the teaching of religion was also carried out.

In the years 1944-1947 the main problems in Lemkovyna were religious issues related to the resettlement of this population. This concerned both deportation to Ukraine, as well as expulsions to the "Recovered Territories" as part of "Operation Vistula"[128].

The resettlements to Ukraine in the years 1944-1946 had a significant impact on the fate of the Orthodox Church in Lemkovyna. These events thoroughly depleted its social and material base. They led to the breakdown of the integrity of parish communities and disrupted the structure of the Orthodox Church created in the interwar period. Before the beginning of deportations there were 42 pastoral centers (parishes and branches) in Lemkovyna. The largest clusters of faithful were grouped into the parishes of: Florynka (approximately 1246 people)[129], Mszana (1200), Polany (1170), Tylawa (950), Świątkowa Wielka (815), Izby (800), Bartne (738), Bogusza (671), Wołowiec (665) Lipowiec (643) and Binczarowa (633).[130]

In order to secure Orthodox structures (including abandoned property), Metropolitan Dionizy entrusted Fr. Witaliusz Sahajdakowski with the post of administrator of the existing parishes in July 1945. In mid-October 1945 he informed the Warsaw Orthodox Spiritual Consistory that in Lemkovyna only 5 parishes with 6 affiliated branches were

---

three Lemko deaneries ceased to exist actually). Attempts to create a deanery in Florynka were made due to the significant distance from Kraków and due to the communication difficulties. Administratively it was supposed to have all parishes in Lemkovyna. It was not created because of the displacements of the Operation "Vistula", see: K. Urban, Z dziejów Kościoła prawosławnego na Łemkowszczyźnie w latach 1945-1947, "Zeszyty Naukowe Akademii Ekonomicznej w Krakowie", no 460, Kraków 1995, p. 101-102.

[128] See more: S. Dudra, Kościół prawosławny na ziemiach zachodnich i północnych po II wojnie światowej, Zielona Góra 2004; P. Gerent, Prawosławie na Dolnym Śląsku w latach 1945-1989, Toruń 2007.

[129] In this number there were the faithful from Wawrzka.

[130] A list of parishes and estimated number of the faithful are given by R. Dubec, Z dziejów parafii prawosławnych na łemkowszczyźnie..., p. 23-206.

conducting activity.[131] Probably these data are incomplete. This resulted, among others, from disastrous traffic conditions and difficulties in reaching most of the villages.[132] The priest W. Sahajdakowski's activity was interrupted in the autumn of 1945. Under pressure from the authorities he was forced to leave Lemkovyna.[133]

It is necessary to mention the attitude of the Orthodox Church authorities towards the deportations in Lemkovyna. On 19 October 1945, the Warsaw Orthodox Spiritual Consistory wrote a letter to the Offices of the Districts of Gorlice and Nowy Sącz on leaving Orthodox Lemkos in those districts. A similar letter was sent to the governor of Rzeszów a few days later.[134] In January and March 1946, Metropolitan Dionizy intervened against the deportation of Orthodox Lemkos in the Ministry of Public Administration.[135] These actions, however, brought no positive results.

Along with the people Orthodox priests were also deported.[136] In

---

[131] Bartne (branch: Przegonina), Florynka (Binczarowa, Wawrzka), Izby (Bieliczna), Królowa Ruska (Bogusza), Uście Ruskie (Kwiatoń). They also planned to reactivate parishes in Banica, Piorunka and Tylawa, see: K. Urban, Z dziejów Kościoła prawosławnego na Łemkowszczyźnie w latach 1945-1947, "Zeszyty Naukowe Akademii Ekonomicznej w Krakowie", no 460, Kraków 1995, p. 104-105.

[132] AAN, MAP, sygn. 1050, The letter of the Provincial Office of Kraków to Religious Department of MAP of 19 May 1945.

[133] W. Sahajdakiwśkyj, Prawdy ne wtopyty. Spohady z 50-tyriczczia pasterstwa 1927-1977, Toronto 1977, p. 142-144.

[134] State Archive in Rzeszów, Provincial Office of Rzeszów, sygn. 466, A letter of WDKP to the District Office in Gorlice of 29 October 1945.

[135] AWMP, Metropolitan Dionizy's letters to the Ministry of Public Administration of 15 January 1946 and 22 March 1946.

[136] Of course, Greek Catholic clergy were also displaced. The authorities saw in this a factor leading to the liquidation of the Greek Catholic rite. Just in April 1945 the hierarchs and part of priests of the Greek Catholic Church were arrested. The situation even worsened after the so-called Lwów Synod (8-10 March 1946), where the Greek Catholic Church was banned in the Soviet Union. The consequence of these developments was the arrest and transfer of Bishop Jozafat Kocyłowski and next his suffragan Bishop Hryhorij Lakota to the Soviet authorities. According to estimates in the years 1944-1946 23 Greek Catholic priests were killed and about 300 were displaced. The institutions and religious organizations of the Church were also liquidated, see: E. Misiło, Hreko-Katołycka Cerkwa w Polszczi (1944-1947), [in:] Ukrajina i Polszcza miż mynułym i majbutnym, Lwiw 1991, p. 105-106; Z. Wojewoda, Zarys historii Kościoła greckokatolickiego w Polsce w latach 1944-1989, Kraków 1994; I. Biłas, Likwidacja Greckokatolickiej Diecezji Przemyskiej oraz tragiczne losy jej ordynariusza biskupa Jazafata Kocyłowskiego w kontekście polityki wyznaniowej ZSRR, [in:] Polska-Ukraina 1000 lat sąsiedztwa, ed. S. Stępień, vol. III, Przemyśl 1996; I. Harasym, Hreko-Katołycka Cerkwa naperedodni ta pislia akciji „Wisła", [in:] U poszukach prawdy pro akciju „Wisła", ed. M. Kozak, Pere-

the autumn of 1945, orders to leave Nowy Sącz district were given to all Orthodox clergy, referring to rules regarding residence in a frontier zone. Among others Bishop Tymoteusz (Szretter) and the Warsaw Orthodox Spiritual Consistory protested against their forced removal.[137] However, by the end of 1945 most of the clergy and the faithful were displaced. Some of them were forced to leave by [the Soviet] People's Commissariat for Internal Affairs (NKVD), including Fr. Aleksander Iwanowicz from Bogusza and Fr. Piotr Taranowski from Florynka. The latter did not escape deportation despite his function as the Orthodox Parish Administrator in Lemkovyna.[138] Willingly or unwillingly they left the parishes, including among others the priests Paweł Libow from Radocyna, Terentij Osadczenko from Skwirtne, Grzegorz Cybulko from Jaszkowa, Mikołaj Kucharuk from Świątkowa Wielka, Onufry Orski from Kwiatoń, Eugeniusz Gryzentowicz from Czarne, Ignacy Kosma from Piorunka and Jerzy Buczyński from Florynka (the replacement parish priest for Fr. P. Taranowski who had been displaced earlier.)[139]

It should also be noted that the number of clergy had already been reduced by the earlier deportation to forced labor in Germany of the parish priest in Tylawa, Fr. Wiktor Masik (in 1942), and by deportations by the Soviet authorities to Kazakhstan of Fr. Antoni Tatiewski (1940-1946) and to Siberia of Fr. Jerzy Pawłyszyn, parish priest in Czarne (he stayed in exile until 1954 and died in the Soviet Union in 1958.) At the beginning of 1946 only two priests conducted pastoral services in Lemkovyna: Fr. Jan Lewiarz (since 1942 the parish priest in Bartne, with branches in Bodaki and Wołowiec) and Fr. Dymitr Chylak (since 1928 the parish priest in Izby and Bieliczna). Although a network of parishes had and faithful who escaped resettlement had been preserved, de facto

myszl 1998, p. 20-21; I. Hałagida, Między Moskwą, Warszawą i Watykanem. Dzieje Kościoła greckokatolickiego w Polsce w latach 1944-1970, Warszawa 2013.

[137] AWMP, A letter of Warsaw Orthodox Spiritual Consistory (WDKP) to the Religious Department of MAP of 12 Novemeber 1945; AAN, MAP, sygn. 1051, A letter of Religious Department of MPA to the Provincial Office in Lublin on the Orthodox clergy of 15 Decmber 1945.

[138] P. Taranowski served as an administrator since September 1944 to 14 July 1945, when he was displaced to Ukraine, see: A. Horobczenko, Mytrofornyj protoijerej Petro Taranowśkyj, "Cerkowny Kalendar", 1996, Sanok 1995, p. 227; J. Zwoliński, J. Merena, Na Łemkowszczyźnie. Floryna (nasze seło), Koszalin 1999, p. 88-89.

[139] Most of them did not come back to Poland. Priests E. Gryzentowicz (1977), J. Buczyński (1982), M. Kucharuk (1983), P. Taranowski (1988) died in the USSR, see: G. Sosna, A. Troc-Sosna, Hierarchia i duchowieństwo Kościoła prawosławnego w granicach II Rzeczypospolitej i Polski powojennej w XIX i XXI wieku, Ryboły 2012.

the pastoral posts in Lemkovyna were deprived of pastoral care.[140]

The situation partly changed with the return of part of the displaced population and people discharged from the Red Army.[141] In addition, the need to secure the property of inactive Orthodox parishes forced the authorities of the Orthodox Church to take steps to settle the problem. On 11 March 1946 Fr. Stefan Biegun arrived in Florynka. He was appointed to handle parishioners in Bogusza and Królowa Ruska.[142] On 7 May 1946 the priests Włodzimierz Wieżański and Wsiewołod Łopuchowicz were sent to Lemkovyna.[143] These activities were supported by the Department of Religious Affairs of the Ministry of Public Administration.[144] On 10 May 1946 Fr. Aleksy Znosko was also delegated to the parish in Czarna, Gorlice district. However, for unknown reasons, he did not arrive in Lemkovyna.[145] In Włodzimierz Wieżański's reports sent to Warsaw Orthodox Theological Consistory there is a lot of interesting information about the situation in Lemkovyna in the final stages of displacement. Fr. Wieżański celebrated worship for the Orthodox population, among others, in Bogusza, Florynka and Piorunka. He also mentioned church services in Banica, Czarne, Śnietnica and Bartne. Assessing his stay in Lemkovyna he wrote: "The moral and religious state of parishes, which I visited, is at a high level. The people move me with their religiosity and

---

[140] Fr. Onufry Sapieha (a parish priest in Wołowiec since 16 October 1944) left Lemkovyna in 1945. After the displacement of most of the faithful he moved to Łódź, where he died in 1952, see: R. Dubec, Z dziejów parafii prawosławnych..., p. 201.

[141] Among others Lemkos from Słotwiny, Królowa Ruska, Bogusza and Florynka voluntarily joined the Red Army. Most Lemkos were conscripted into the army their number should be estimated at approx. 500 people, see: M. Doński, Wkład Łemków w walkę z okupantem hitlerowskim, [in:] Z myślą o Polsce Ludowej, Rzeszów 1963, p. 308-309; J. Kwiek, Żydzi, Łemkowie, Słowacy w województwie krakowskim w latach 1945-1949/50, Kraków 1998, p. 101-109.

[142] The priest stayed in Florynka only till 19 May 1946. He was forced to leave under pressure from the local authorities. However, he escaped the deportation to Ukraine. He returned again to Florynka only in July 1947, see: K. Urban, Ks. Stefan Biegun (1903-1983) zapis jednego życia..., p. 16-18.

[143] AWMP, The resolution of WDKP of 7 May 1946. Fr. W. Wieżański was to take care of the religious population in the parishes of Banica and Piorunka (district Nowy Sącz), and in other places where there were no Orthodox priests. Fr. Łopuchowicz did not fulfill his mission, because he was turned back from the way to Lemkivshchyna by the authorities from Nowy Sącz, see: K. Urban, Z dziejów Kościoła Prawosławnego na Łemkowszczyźnie (Raport ks. Wieżańskiego z pobytu na Łemkowszczyźnie w maju 1946 roku), "Cerkiewny Wiestnik", 1991, no 7, p. 31.

[144] AAN, MAP, sygn. 1047, A letter of WDKP to the Religious Department of MAP of 10 May 1946.

[145] Fr. A. Znosko serviced in Wrocław since 8 December 1946.

devotion to the Orthodox rite."[146]

On 25 May 1946 Fr. Antoni Tatiewski (he worked in Królowa Ruska and Bogusza and managed to organize parishes in Piorunka and Banica) was sent to the Nowy Sącz district.[147] In addition, on 16 July Fr. Michał Popiel was sent the area of Gorlice district; he knew Lemkovyna well (among others in the years 1928-1931 he served in Hyrowa, Mszana, Tylawa, Polany, Lipowiec, and Florynka.) He took over the parish in Uście Ruskie and Kwiatoń and also worked in Skwirtne and Regetów.

In May 1946, the Warsaw Orthodox Spiritual Consistory informed the Religious Department of the Ministry of Public Administration that the overwhelming majority of Orthodox parishes existing in Lemkovyna were currently liquidated (mentioned among others were Ciechanie, Chyrowa, Czarne, Desznica, Grab, Kamianna, Lipowiec, Milik, Mszana, Radocyna, Skwirtne, Śnietnica, Świątkowa Wielka, Wołowiec and Uście Ruskie.)[148]

As a result of the resettlements to Ukraine, religious life in Lemkovyna became disorganized. Orthodox priests themselves were not knowledgeable about how many priests were doing pastoral service and in which parishes; Fr. J. Lewiarz pointed this out in reports sent to Warsaw.[149] Several clerics led a campaign for protecting abandoned Orthodox property and providing ministry to the remaining Orthodox people. Still, the main problem was a lack of clergy, who left due to threats posed by various military units. Among others, Fr. Jan Gachowicz, who was delegated to Lemkovyna in September 1946, and took over the parish in Wołowiec, left after a few weeks. On 25 May 1946, Fr. Antoni Tatiewski had taken over the parish in Bogusza, but in December of that year he was forced to leave Lemkovyna or suffer the death penalty.[150] The shortage of clergy led to reduction of religious life among the rest of the population. Church services were celebrated sporadically, often once a month, and catechesis

---

[146] K. Urban, Z dziejów Kościoła prawosławnego na Łemkowszczyźnie (Raport ks. Wieżańskiego z pobytu na Łemkowszczyźnie w maju 1946 roku), "Cerkiewny Wiestnik", 1991, no 7, p. 37.

[147] Fr. A. Tatiewski was a parish priest in Ciechanie in 1937-1939. In 1940 he was deported to the Soviet Union, and came back to Poland in 1946, see: D. Rusynko, A. Barna, Piorunka-Perunka i jej mieszkańcy, Legnica 2007, p. 136-137.

[148] AAN, MAP, sygn. 1047, A letter of WDKP to the Religious Department of MAP of 10 May 1946.

[149] K. Urban, Z dziejów Kościoła prawosławnego na Łemkowszczyźnie w latach 1945-1947 (Raporty ks. Jana Lewiarza z parafii Bartne), "Cerkiewny Wiestnik", 1991, no 11, p. 39.

[150] AWMP, Fr. Antoni Tatiewski's report to Metropolitan Dionizy of 6 January 1947.

for children and young people were essentially confined to the places where a priest resided.

During this period, it was difficult to determine the number of faithful in the Lemko parishes. At the beginning of 1947 there were officially eight parishes with 19 branches in Lemkovyna, and estimates of between 3500 and 4500 Orthodox believers there.[151] It seems that these figures, however, were overstated. Pastoral posts existed, but were deprived of both faithful and clergy.

In order to strengthen the staff of the clergy in January 1947 the Warsaw Orthodox Spiritual Consistory planned to send Fr. Serafin (Samojlik) to Lemkovyna. This priest because of unknown reasons failed to fulfill his mission. Eventually, Fr. Aleksy Nestorowicz[152] and Fr. Mikołaj Kostyszyn were delegated to the Lemko parishes.[153]

The fate of the Orthodox Church in Lemkovyna was sealed with "Operation Vistula". The displacement of the Orthodox population began in late May and June 1947. By the end of that period parishes in western Lemkovyna had ceased to function. Fr. Stefan Biegun in his report to Metropolitan Dionizy of 21 July 1947 stated that "all Orthodox parishes in the western part of Lemkovyna were liquidated during the month of June this year because of the displacement of the Lemko people by the Polish Army."[154] Basically, by the end of July Orthodox religious life in the area had ceased to exist. The Roman Catholic Church tried to take over "emptiness". Already in July 1947, the Vicar General of the Roman Catholic Curia in Tarnów, Fr. Karol Pękala asked the provincial authorities to agree on the establishment of Roman Catholic parishes in the districts of Nowy Sącz, Nowy Targ and Gorlice.[155] Some of the abandoned, post-Lemko Orthodox churches were acquired by the Roman Catholic Church, while others were devastated and completely destroyed.

The Orthodox clergy were deported along with the faithful. Six priests

---

[151] About the situation in the Orthodox Church during the Operation "Vistula" see: G. Kuprianowicz, Akcja „Wisła" a Kościół prawosławny, [in:] Akcja „Wisła", ed. J. Pisuliński, Warszawa 2003.

[152] Fr. A. Nestorowicz was ordained on March 23 1947 and directly sent as a temporary administrator of the parish in Bogusza. He serviced there until 1 July 1947.

[153] Fr. M. Kostyszyn serviced in the parish in Piorunka (district Nowy Sącz), AWMP, A letter of WDKP to Fr. S. Biegun of 6 May 1947.

[154] AWMP, Fr. S. Biegun report to Metropolitan Dionizy of 21 January 1947.

[155] AAN, MAP, sygn. 1047, The letter of Religious Department of the Ministry of Public Administration to the Governor of Kraków on 2 August 1947.

were expelled from Lemkovyna: Dymitr Chylak, Jan Lewiarz, Michał Popiel, Mikołaj Kostyszyn and Aleksy Nesterowicz. Fr. Stefan Biegun, the last Orthodox priest in the region, left the parish in Florynka on 3 July 1947.[156]

After 1947, Orthodox Church authorities couldn't maintain church life in Lemkovyna. As a result of resettlement, Orthodox parishes ceased to exist. The displaced population began construction of new parish structures in the Recovered Territories, thanks to the support of the clergy and Orthodox authorities, including the personal intervention of Metropolitan Dionizy. In Lemkovyna, Orthodoxy began to recover only in the second half of the 1950s.

---

[156] K. Urban, Ks. Stefan Biegun. Zapis jednego życia..., p. 18.

Church in Jasionka

CHAPTER 3

Two parishes – two conflicts: Rozdziele and Polany as examples of state policy towards Orthodoxy in Lemkovyna

Upon completion of the "Operation Vistula" all the Orthodox parishes in Lemkovyna were liquidated. The Orthodox Church lost most of its material assets. Many historic churches and chapels were destroyed, and some of them were desecrated. For example, local authorities turned the churches in Kwiatoń, Regetów and Wysowa into storehouses, and those in Bartne, Blechnarka, Gładyszów and Wołowiec into stables for cattle and hogs. The Orthodox church in Bodaki was turned into a barn and soldiers from the army border guards arranged a toilet in the chapel on Mount Jawor[157]. As well, many parish cemeteries, valuable and ancient Orthodox icons and accessories were destroyed and desecrated.

Religious life in Lemkovyna began to recover after 1956[158]. This was due to the progressive liberalization of policy of the Polish authorities, which resulted in the possibility for some of those displaced in "Operation Vistula" to return. They made efforts to create their own parishes. By autumn 1956 Fr. Jan Lewiarz began celebrating services in Bartne. One year later a parish in Bodaki was founded, and in 1958 worship began in Blechnarka, Hańczowa and Wołowiec[159].

At the same time, the authorities made it difficult to open new pastoral

---

[157] See: A. Radziukiewicz, Rewolucja w duszy, "Przegląd Prawosławny", 1994, no 8, p. 11-15.

[158] In 1951 after the reorganization of the diocesan structure by Metropolitan Makary Lemkovyna became a part of the Diocese of Łódź and Poznań, then under the adjustment made by the Council of Bishops PAKP on 30 April 1958 was incorporated into the Diocese of Warszawa-Bielsk. Since 1983 the Orthodox parishes have been in the newly erected Diocese of Przemyśl-Nowy Sącz, whose Ordinary Bishop is the Archbishop Adam (Dubec).

[159] Moreover, in the '60s, among others, parishes in Pielgrzymka, Komańcza, Turzańsk, Szczawne, Bielanka, Kunkowa, Gładyszów, Leszczyny, Konieczna, Regetów, Zdynia and St. Mount Jawor were created.

points. They did not grant permission for the erection of pastoral institutions, including ones in Hańczowa, Nowica, Tylawa and Uście Gorlickie. Thereby the development of Orthodox religious life in Lemkovyna faced serious obstacles. Issues associated with the years-long efforts to create a parish in Rozdziele and the religious situation in Polany were also part of the process.

Rozdziele: Three decades of efforts to have a house of worship

The long-term efforts needed to create a Orthodox parish in Rozdziele (1958-1984) illustrate the attitude and reflect the policy of state authorities towards the activities of the Orthodox Church in Lemkovyna.[160] The ordeal of the faithful from Rozdziele, Wapienne and Macyna was characteristic of many Orthodox communities returning to his homeland after 1956. Actions taken by the Office for Religious Affairs in Warsaw and the Department for Religious Affairs in Rzeszów was a derivative of an overall policy aimed at reducing the development of religious life national minorities in Poland.

The entire process of creating a pastoral place in Rozdziele by the Lemko Orthodox community should also be considered in this context. This town was founded in the sixteenth century on the site of a previously-organized, but then-abandoned part of the village of Lipinki. In 1885 it consisted of 547 people, including 507 Greek Catholics, 35 Roman Catholics and 3 Jews.[161] In the interwar period the Greek Catholic parish of the Nativity of the Blessed Virgin Mary functioned there. Administratively it belonged to the Deanery of Gorlice (Przemyśl diocese), and since 1934 it belonged to the Apostolic Administration for Lemkovyna. In 1936, the parish had 690 people (faithful from neighboring towns, including Bednarka and Wapienne also belonged to it). The faithful prayed in a church built in 1786, which after 1947 was used as a branch church by the Roman Catholic parish in Lipinki. As a result of "Operation Vistula"

[160] The religious policy of the state since 1945, see: R. Michalak, Polityka wyznaniowa państwa polskiego wobec mniejszości religijnych w latach 1945-1989, Zielona Góra 2014.
[161] J. Żak, A. Piecuch, Łemkowskie cerkwie, Warszawa 2011, p. 243.

approximately 350 Lemkos were displaced from Rozdziele[162].

The first attempts to erect an Orthodox pastoral station in Rozdziele were made in March 1958. Due to the return of some of the displaced people, Fr. Jan Lewiarz, the authority of the Polish Autocephalous Orthodox Church, made efforts to obtain consent to share the Roman Catholic houses of worship, "occasionally used by Catholics."[163] Despite the refusal of church authorities, Orthodox clergy occasionally prayed in the churchyard square. It should be emphasized that it was the very same Lemkos who, before "Operation Vistula" were the faithful of the local Greek Catholic Church, that were supposed to constitute the future Orthodox parish.

Intensive efforts to establish an Orthodox parish in Rozdziele were made in the 1960s. On 4 January 1961, Fr. Jan Lewiarz intervened regarding allocation of the church for the Orthodox community. Again, this issue was settled negatively. The Department for Religious Affairs in Rzeszów did not agree "because the church is used by the Roman Catholic Church."[164] Fr. Lewiarz again undertook efforts in the matter on 14 September 1961. Metropolitan Tymoteusz (Szretter) also intervened in this case on 6 October 1961. A negative decision was issued by the Office for Religious Affairs on 12 November 1961[165].

In the second half of the 1960s the residents of Rozdziele took the initiative themselves. On 8 February 1966 they turned to the Dean of the Deanery of Rzeszów, Fr. Jan Lewiarz, "asking for assignment of an

---

[162] They were forced to settle in the western lands, mostly in the area of contemporary districts: Szprotawa and Głogów. Later, due to difficulties with erection of the Greek Catholic pastoral centers, they were the creators of Orthodox parishes, among others, in Przemków (1949) and in Leszno Górne (1954). In 1954 they also took part in an attempt to create a Greek Catholic parish in Leszno Dolne (district Szprotawa). In 1961, among others, Greek Catholics from Rozdziele became a group of Christians that led to creating a parish in Szprotawa.

[163] AAN, Office for Religious Affairs (UdSW), The Department of Non-Catholic Faiths, sygn. 131/423, Calendar of events in Rozdziele from 1958 to 31 December 1971.

[164] Ibidem, sygn. 131/398, Letters of Fr. J. Lewiarz to Presidium of Provincial National Council (PWRN) The Department of Religiuos Affairs in Rzeszów on 4 January and 14 September 1961, ibidem, Letters of PWRN in Rzeszów to Fr. J. Lewiarz on 21 January and 6 October 1961.

[165] Ibidem, sygn. 75/5, Letter of Metropolitan Tymoteusz to UdSW on 6 October 1961. Letter of UdSW to the Office of the Metropolitan on 12 November 1961. The argument was the same as in the case of the Department of Religious Affairs in Rzeszów.

Orthodox priest and provision of constant pastoral care."[166] In 1966, the issue of the parish in Rozdziele once again became a subject of interest to the Office for Religious Affairs, which had intervened many times, in this case with the religious authorities in Rzeszów[167]. Metropolitan Stefan also intervened in this case. In 1967 in his letters to the Office of Religious Affairs he stated that "in Rozdziele there are 22 Orthodox, 16 Roman Catholic and 9 mixed families. Moreover, in the surrounding villages of Wapienne there are 14 Orthodox families, in Bednarka 3 and Macyna 2 Orthodox people"[168]. The authorities also stressed that "79 people of the Orthodox faith lived [in Rozdziele], and in Wapienne 48 people. In addition, 3 Orthodox families from Wola Cieklińska, 9 families from Bednarka, 4 families from Folusz and approximately 50 families from Gorlice would go to the church. All of the above villages would constitute one parish in Rozdziele."[169]

These efforts of the 1960s aimed at providing an Orthodox house of worship did not achieve their intended purpose. The reason was, among others, the fact that the Roman Catholic parish priest "always pointed out the negative position of the diocesan curia in Tarnów." It can be assumed that the state authorities themselves, both at central and local levels, were not interested in the ultimate solution to the problem.

Due to emerging conflicts among the faithful the temple was closed and sealed at the beginning of 1969. However, as early as 6 February 1969 Catholics "entered the church through a side door, and the vicar of the parish in Lipinki, Fr. Józef Puchała, celebrated a service." On 14 February the district authorities in Gorlice, after talks with Orthodox (Fr. J. Lewiarz) and Roman Catholic (Fr. Franciszek Borowiec) priests, took the position that "the church may be made available for worship purposes, provided that there is joint use by both religions, because otherwise it will be closed. The concept of sharing a church was also presented: on the

---

[166] Ibidem, Letter of inhabitants of Rozdziele to the Dean of the Orthodox Deanery in Sanok on 8 February 1966.

[167] Ibidem, sygn. 131/423, Letters of UdSW to Presidium of Provincial National Council in Rzeszów on 123 April, 7 June, 30 June, 25 July, 19 August, 4 November, and 14 December 1966.

[168] Ibidem, Letters of Metropolitan Tymoteusz to UdSW on 21 January, 16 August, and 4 November 1967.

[169] Ibidem, Information Presidium of Provincial National Council in Rzeszów about the religious and nationalistic situation in Rozdziele in connection with the closure of the Orthodox chutrch by the Presidium of National District Council in Gorlice on 29 October 1971.

first Sunday of the month by followers of the Orthodox Church, on other Sundays by Roman Catholics; major Church feasts will be celebrated by each confession at their time."[170]

On 3 March 1969 the Orthodox faithful, in accordance with previous findings, came to the Roman Catholic sacristan to get the keys to enter the building. The request was denied so "they entered by force and began the service." It was disturbed by the Catholic population, who, along with the priest, removed the Orthodox. They also did not obtain the permission for the celebration of the liturgy during the Easter holidays. In the meantime, there were burglaries and devastation of the church. Both Orthodox and Catholics took part in those incidents.

In December 1969 there was a worsening of the conflict between the faithful. In their aftermath Fr. Mikołaj Słokotowicz was beaten (14 December) and a pregnant Orthodox woman was roughed up (22 December). As a result, she miscarried.[171]

These developments led to the closure and sealing of the building on 19 January 1970.[172] The provincial authorities took the view that "the church may be made available for the purposes of worship, provided in common use by the Roman Catholic and Orthodox believers."[173] Despite the building's sealing, people were systematically breaking the seal. Catholic services were celebrated in the Orthodox church. The Diocesan Curia in Tarnów demanded the returning of the building to Catholics, while refusing to share with the Orthodox, because "it would be an approval of the violence which they have committed."[174]

On 19 May 1971 the Department for Religious Affairs in Rzeszów pointed out that the church in Rozdziele "may be made available for the purpose of worship provided there is common use by the Roman

---

[170] Ibidem, sygn. 131/423, Information of Presidium of Provincial National Council in Rzeszów about the religious and nationalistic situation in Rozdziele in connection with the closure of the Orthodox church by the Presidium of National District Council in Gorlice on 29 October 1971.

[171] Ibidem, Calendar of events in Rozdziele from 1958 to 31 December 1971.

[172] Archives of The Institue of National Rememberance (AIPN), BU 01283/1659, Letter of Citizen's Militia (MO) Headquarters of Province Rzeszów to the Head of the Department III Dep. IV Ministry of Internal Affairs on 4 February 1970.

[173] AAN, UdSW, The Department of Non-Catholic Faiths, sygn. 131/423, Letter of the Department of Religious Affairs of Presidium of Provincial National Council in Rzeszów on 19 May 1971.

[174] AIPN, BU 01283/1659, Letter of Diocese Curia in Tarnów to Presidium of Provincial National Council in Rzeszów on 24 January 1970.

Catholic and Orthodox followers."[175] On 26 August 1971 the provincial
authorities presented a proposal for joint use of the building again. They
proposed that the Orthodox Church would use it on the first Sunday of
the month (and on major holidays and funerals), and on the remaining
days the church would be at the disposal of the Roman Catholic Church.
The maintenance costs were to be borne proportionately by both parties.
At the same time, it stated that in case of disobedience to this decision
the situation would be reset to the situation before 1966 (i.e., the church
would be at the sole disposal of the Roman Catholic Church).

In autumn 1971 further discussions on sharing the building were carried out. On 14 October representatives of the Catholic and Orthodox
parties met in the Presidium of the District National Council in Gorlice;
"unfortunately the Catholic side did not show good will and a settlement was not reached." On 4 November talks between Bishop Aleksy
(the suffragan of Metropolitan Bazyli) and Bishop Jerzy Ablewicz (the
Ordinary [Bishop] of the Diocese of Tarnów) were held at the Presidium
of the Provincial National Council in Rzeszów. The Catholic party did not
agree to sharing the building on the terms of agreed days and hours to
celebrate religious services "because it will come to fussing and fighting in
the church". In addition, Bishop Jerzy Ablewicz "described the Orthodox
clergy as having no qualifications to be [...] a Roman Catholic partner."[176]
In the above atmosphere of the talks the issue was not resolved again.

In the early 1970s the Orthodox took more action in order to erect
a parish in Rozdziele. They had high hopes for the new government of
Edward Gierek and a possible change in government policy towards the
Orthodox Church. They turned, among others, to Prime Minister Piotr
Jaroszewicz, to the Office for Religious Affairs, the Central Committee
of The Polish United Workers' Party in Warsaw and the Chairman of
the Council of State Henryk Jabłoński. It was recognized that disputes
between Catholics and Orthodox at the level of local authorities were
often dealt with unfavorably for the Orthodox side[177].

[175] "Wiadomości PAKP", 1972, no 2, p. 67-68.
[176] AAN, UdSW, The Department of Non-Catholic Faiths, sygn. 131/423, Information
of Presidium of Provincial National Council in Rzeszów about the religious and
nationalistic situation in Rozdziele in connection with the closure of the Orthodox
church by the Presidium of National District Council in Gorlice on 29 October 1971;
ibidem, Information of Presidium of Provincial National Council in Rzeszów about
the situation in Rozdziele on 5 November 1971.
[177] Ibidem, Letter of Fr. A Dubec to Metropolitan Bazyli on 27 March 1972.

The new [Orthodox] Archbishop Bazyli (Doroszkiewicz) tried to solve the problem of the faithful from Rozdziele. In letters sent to the Office for Religious Affairs (22 October 1970, 25 February 1971, 7 March 1972) and the Presidium of the Presidium of the Provincial National Council in Rzeszów (3 July 1971) he emphasized "the need for rapid and satisfactory settlement of the matter of the Orthodox asking for over ten years about the possibility of celebrating their own worship." The hierarch also addressed this issue in correspondence with the Polish Primate, Cardinal Stefan Wyszyński.[178]

Activities were also continued by the [Orthodox] dean of Rzeszów Fr. Aleksander Dubec[179]. In 1972 there was even the concept of building a [new] Orthodox church in Rozdziele. However, due to the reluctance of the faithful the project was postponed. In the opinion of Fr. A. Dubec "the faithful in Rozdziele and Wapienne are highly concerned, devastated and disheartened by the fact of lawlessness which is currently [see below] taking place in Polany." They stated further that "a [new] church building will not be built because our church stands, and is in good condition [...] We built it and there is not a single Roman Catholic brick in it. It is our work and our property. Our fathers, as they were forced to accept the Union, contributed not only the church, but also residential and business buildings and land. We are returning now to the bosom of the Orthodox Church, and we have been asking for return of the building for 13 years."[180]

The task of creating an Orthodox parish in Rozdziele ended successfully only in the mid-80s. The creation of the [Orthodox] Diocese of Przemyśl-Nowy Sącz in 1983 had a significant influence. Creation of a new eparchy resulted in greater opportunities to set up new pastoral points (including parishes erected in Zyndranowa and Gorlice).

After 27 years of effort, worship in Rozdziele started in 1985 (the parish itself was officially created on 25 September 1984.)[181] Fr. Jan Lewiarz was

---

[178] Extensive documentation [in:] AAN, UdSW, The Department of Non-Catholic Faiths, sygn. 131/423; see also: Letter of Metropolitan Bazyli to the Polish Primate Cardinal Wyszyński of 31 December 1971, "Wiadomości PAKP", 1972, no 2, p. 67-68.

[179] AAN, UdSW, The Department of Non-Catholic Faiths, sygn. 131/404, Letter of dean in Rzeszow Fr A. Dubec to PWRN in Rzeszów of 23 November 1971.

[180] Ibidem, sygn. 131/413, Letter of Fr. A Dubec to Metropolitan Bazyli of 27 March 1972.

[181] R. Dubec, 25 lat parafii w Rozdzielu, "Wiadomości PAKP", 2009, no 11, p. 10; P. Trochanowski, Wertania z rozdilenych dorich, "Cerkownyj Kalendar", 1987, p. 122-

appointed the first parish priest. A wooden building, dating back to 1785, serving the Orthodox Church, was moved from Serednica near Ustrzyki Dolne. The ceremonial consecration of this church, dedicated to the Nativity of the Blessed Virgin Mary, was held on 24 August 1986. It is a subsidiary of the parish in Pielgrzymka and part of the Deanery of Sanok.

Among the faithful:
The dispute over the church in Polany

The case of Polany, concerning a dispute of the faithful (Greek Catholics, Orthodox and Roman Catholics) over the church there, electrified the concerned communities for decades. It became a symbol of division and inability to resolve the issue. Janusz L. Sobolewski wrote that "you can look at Polany as a battlefield of two Christian churches. Too many words and deeds confirm this fact, so everyone must notice the mutual blows; too much bile and too many tears were poured out to bring the dispute in Polany to inter-parish war."[182]

The church in Polany was built by Greek Catholics in 1913. During the Second Polish Republic part of the population of Polany returned to Orthodoxy. "Above all the awareness that we have always been Orthodox"[183] prevailed. Already in 1927 the Council of Bishops of the Orthodox Church tried to normalize the legal situation of pastoral centers which arose in Lemkovyna, including the one in Polany. They wanted primarily to give them the status of parishes and the delegated priest the rights of civil registrars and catechists [i.e. paid government employees.][184]

During World War II, the church in Polany was significantly damaged. About 50 families remained in the village after the deportations to Ukraine (1944-1946) and to the western and northern parts of Poland under "Operation Vistula" (1947). Since 1947 "no one here has mentioned

---

129.

[182] J. L. Sobolewski, Spór o cerkiew, "Życie Literackie", 1983, no 17, p. 8; about the conflict in Polany see: S. Dudra, Cerkiew w Polanach. Z dziejów konfliktu wyznaniowego na Łemkowszczyźnie, "Rocznik Ruskiej Bursy 2009", Gorlice 2009, p. 65-78.

[183] R. Dubec, Powrót Łemków do prawosławia w odrodzonej Rzeczypospolitej Polskiej (1926-1939), part 2, Apostolska Administracja Łemkowszczyzny jako próba zahamowania konwersji, "Cerkiewny Wiestnik", 2006, no 2, p. 51.

[184] The draft sent to the Ministry of Religious Affairs and Public Enlightenment lists the 9 parishes, including not manned outpost in Polany, AAN, MWRiOP, sygn. 1043.

Orthodoxy or Greek Catholicism aloud. We all take part in Roman Catholic services. Polany is a branch of the Roman Catholic parish in Myscowa."[185]

In Polany, due to extensive damage to the church, Roman Catholic services were held in private homes, in which shrines were devised for household worship (e.g. at the home of the Cynkiel and Zięba family.) In 1962 they also began to use "a wooden canopy protecting the priest from the rain and wind which had been built by the Roman Catholic-Uniate priest Wysoczański. In this way, a kind of status quo was established in the village. Roman Catholics celebrated masses in two places: during the winter, in Maria Zięba's house; during the summer, in front of a wooden chapel on the church square."[186]

In 1966 the former Greek Catholic church in Polany was not being used. It was in poor condition and required major refurbishment. The initiator of the restoration of the church was Jan Gałczyk.[187] The revival of Orthodoxy in Lemkovyna after 1956 also affected the situation in Polany. Efforts to erect a parish there were taken on 11 February 1961. However, on 18 February 1961, the Office for Religious Affairs gave a negative decision in this case.[188] According to the Department for Religious Affairs of the Presidium of the Provincial National Council in Rzeszów, "the country's population does not want the Orthodox Church, and seeks at all costs to organize a Greek Catholic church."[189]

Finally, the actions of the faithful in Polany, also supported by the Orthodox Church in Warsaw, were successful. On 24 February 1966 the post-Uniate building was transferred to the Orthodox Church, and on 16 June 1966 the authorities agreed on the creation of the Orthodox parish in Polany.[190] Fr. Michał Rydzanicz was appointed the parish priest (he served

---

[185] M. Bołtryk, Duma Łemków, [in:] A. Radziukiewicz, M. Bołtryk, Precz z mnichami, Białystok 1995, p. 77.

[186] J. L. Sobolewski, op. cit.

[187] Fr. Michał Rydzanicz took up the issue of erecting the parish, see: M. Bołtryk, Duma Łemków..., p. 78.

[188] AAN, UdSW, The Department of Non-Catholic Faiths, sygn. 75/5, Letter of Archbishop Tymoteusz to The Office for Religious Affairs of 11 February 1961, ibidem, Letter of The Office for Religious Affairs to Metropolitan Tymoteusz of 18 February 1961.

[189] Ibidem, Letter of Presidium of Provincial National Council in Rzeszów of 4 August 1961.

[190] Ibidem, sygn. 74/5, Acceptance protocol of 24 February 1966. On behalf of PAKP Fr. Jan Lewiarz took over the temple, ibidem, Letter of the Department for Reli-

there in 1966-1967). Due to the extensive damage, efforts were made to obtain permission to carry out safety work and repairs. The Church Renovation Committee (Jan Gałczyk– chairman, Piotr Myszkowski– treasurer, Mikołaj Bendas– Chairman of the Audit Committee and members Anna Buriak, Piotr Kędzierawski, Jan Myszkowski and Jan Seńczak), which was selected from among the parishioners, supervised the work.

In the years 1966-1971 a major overhaul of the building was carried out. Windows were placed and glassed, the sacristy was plastered, and the church square was fenced. They also filled the "breaches in the walls, a vault of roof trusses was made, the domes were rebuilt and the whole roof was covered with sheet metal. The total cost of the renovation amounted to over 1 million zlotys. This sum, huge for those times, was collected due to efforts of the authorities of the Orthodox Church, the faithful of Polany and other regions of the country and the Orthodox faithful from abroad."[191] Renovation work was supervised by the new parish priest, Fr. Anatol Fedoruk (served 1967-1971).

Immediately after the transfer of the church to the Orthodox Church Roman Catholic priests began an operation in order to prevent the functioning of the parish. They fomented sentiments of hostility, preached "sermons calling for religious and ethnic antagonism", also they even used "threats that no one dared to go to the Orthodox church as it is a pagan, schismatic, and Muscovite faith, and an Orthodox priest is a person specially sent by the party and government to destroy the Roman Catholic faith. Fr. Jan Wysoczański [...] went so far against the Orthodox that penitents were forced by him to take an oath and promises that they would never go to the Orthodox church."[192]

The hotbed of the future conflict was a small "wooden chapel" built on the church square and used by Roman Catholics and Greek Catholics.[193]

---

gious Affairs of PWRN in Rzeszów of 16 June 1966.

[191] Ibidem, sygn. 132/215, Letter of parishioners of the Orthodox parish in Polany to Fr. Primate Józef Glemp of 23 November 1985. The letter of the same content was also addressed to the Office for Religious Affairs, Ordinary of the Diocese of Przemyśl, Bishop Ignacy Tokarczuk, Metropolitan of Warszawa and the whole Poland Bazyli and the Ordinary of the Diocese Przemyśl-Nowy Sącz Fr. Bishop Adam.

[192] Ibidem, sygn. 131/421, Letter of Teodor Gocz to Regional Committee PZPR The Committee for Nationalistic Affairs in Rzeszów of 20 February 1967, also: The report of Fr. A. Fiedoruk to Fr. A. Dubec of 12 September 1967.

[193] It was a "crib compacted provisionally with rough-hewn planks covered with tar paper, dingy, measuring approx. 1.5 m to 2 m", leaving it was not foreseen in the handover protocol of 1966, but it belonged to the Orthodox parish limits after

A decision on the demolition of the building or its removal to another location was issued due to the already emerging conflict between the faithful.[194] In 1969, Roman Catholics and Greek Catholics bought a room where they organized a chapel and catechetical site. After autumn 1970 they had completely stopped celebrating worship in the former chapel.

On 16 April 1971 Fr. A. Fiedoruk issued an order to dismantle the building.[195] These actions led to accusations of desecration and triggered a mood of hostility, which consequently caused of beating of an Orthodox resident, Teodor Bugiel.[196] The conflict was resolved after the arrival of a group of the Citizen's Militia (MO) [police] from Krosno.

On 25 April 1971 an Orthodox liturgy was celebrated in the church. A few hours later, a Catholic service was celebrated near the Orthodox church.[197] Acts of violence and intrusion into the church were made by

fencing off the Orthodox church square, AAN, UdSW, The Department of Non-Catholic Faiths, sygn. 131/421, Letters of Fr A. Fiedoruk to the Ordinary of the Diocese of Przemyśl Fr. Bishop Tokarczuk of 19 April 1971 and to UdSW of 3 May 1971. According to the minutes of the meeting of Community National Council of 24 September 1968 "5 meters from the church there is a Roman Catholic chapel, which is set illegally on the property of the Orthodox parish. It is not conducive to the public safety of persons not employed in the construction of the church but taking part in religious services. These people are exposed to the risk of injury", see: The minutes of the meeting of the Presidium of Community National Council (GRN) in Polany of 24 September 1968, AAN, UdSW, The Department of Non-Catholic Faiths, sygn. 131/421.

[194] Community National Council Bureau decision in Polany of 24 September 1968, the deadline was set for 28 September 1968. AAN, UdSW, The Department of Non-Catholic Faiths, sygn. 131/421, Ibidem, Letter of A. Fiedoruk to UdSW of 3 May 1971.

[195] Previously, the information was posted so that the chapel was moved to another location within seven days. However, the card with information was torn and no action was taken in that case. Contained therein Latin utensils (according to Fr. Fiedoruk they were placed there a few days before the announced demolition of the chapel), were given to the guardian of Roman Catholic chapel in Polany with the participation of an officer MO, AAN, UdSW, The Department of Non-Catholic Faiths, sygn. 131/421, Letter of A. Fiedoruk to UdSW of 3 May 1971. According the information PWRN in Rzeszów at night the chapel was demolished, but it is not known by whom", Ibidem, Information of Presidium of PWRN in Rzeszów of 30 April 1971.

[196] Teodor Bugiel, suffered, among others, from broken ribs, beating the head, numerous swellings of the body. The case went to court. However, in Krosno District Court three persons were acquitted and one punished with 5 month detention in suspension, AAN, UdSW, The Department of Non-Catholic Faiths, sygn. 131/421, Letter of parish priests of Deanery Rzeszów to UdSW of 20 April 1973.

[197] According to the information "devotions were held peacefully and without any interruption. In Polany there is apparent peace", AAN, UdSW, The Department of

the Roman Catholic faithful. They began to occur again in the summer of 1971. On 18 July they invaded a wedding feast and beat Orthodox wedding guests[198]. Roman Catholics said: "There should not be any Orthodox people in Polany [...] Two faiths in one village is too much"[199].

In August and September 1971 there were further incidents. Roman Catholic faithful broke into the locked church square several times "breaking the locks on the fence. They entered the square and celebrated Church services demonstratively. After their departure the Orthodox came and celebrate their devotions inside the church. After its completion, they locked the fence with previously prepared new padlocks and staples."[200] The situation was repeated on consecutive Sundays in September, October and November 1971. During this time there was ever more aggressive behavior by the faithful.

On 28 November 1971 a group of the faithful (about 150 persons) from neighboring villages "under the leadership of Fr. Kazimierz Pańczyszyn" broke into the church. There was desecration, "they demolished the altar, which was thrown into the field." Then a "sacrificial" service was celebrated there. When the temple was occupied by the Roman Catholic Church, the church furnishings and building materials gathered to build a presbytery were also taken (including approximately 20,000 bricks and 25 cubic meters of lumber.) According to a report by the dean of the Orthodox District of Rzeszów, "the act of injustice was done in a previously planned and organized way, and the Orthodox population of Polany does not preclude that it happened with the quiet support of local authorities."[201]

On 30 November 1971 Polish Autocephalous Orthodox Church authorities sent a note to the [Catholic] Primate Cardinal Stefan Wyszyński. It expressed their "protest against unbelievable and scandalous, especially in the era of ecumenism, lawlessness and violation of the

---

Non-Catholic Faiths, sygn. 131/421, Information of Presidium of WRN in Rzeszów of 30 April 1971.

[198] Ibidem, Letter of parish priests of Deanery Rzeszów to UdSW of 20 April 1973.

[199] A. Radziukiewicz, M. Bołtryk, op. cit., p. 80.

[200] J. L. Sobolewski, op. cit.

[201] AAN, UdSW, The Department of Non-Catholic Faiths, sygn. 132/215, Letter of parishioners of the Orthodox parish in Polany to Fr. Primate Józef Glemp of 23 November 1985; ibidem, sygn. 131/421, Report of Fr. A. Dubec to Metropolitan Bazyli of 29 November 1971.

constitutional rights of our Homeland."[202]

Due to inaction of local authorities (neither the Presidium of the National District Council in Krosno, nor the District Headquarters of MO intervened in this matter) "formal religious war broke out"[203] in Polany in December 1971. The Orthodox occupied the building on 7 December. Once inside they found " the sacred altar a mess and the holy antimension had been thrown down and lay at the side of the altar."[204] However, on 8 December 1971 the doors were "shattered and broken by Catholics, who then celebrated a service". On the same day the church was again occupied by the Orthodox who "barricaded themselves in it". There was a siege of the building by Catholics and they raised hostile shouts. Only in the evening did representatives of the local authorities arrive. They decided to close the church temporarily, pending clarification of the situation.

However, on 9 December Catholics and Greek Catholics under the leadership of Fr. K. Pańczyszyn again "with axes and crowbars proceeded to demolish the door [...] after breaking through it they forced their way into the church." They hung their padlock on the door. After several hours, the Orthodox occupied the church for the second time. There were "fights and scuffles among the faithful." Finally, the event ended up with the sealing of the front door and side panels. The keys were cast for "the chairman of the village People's Council (GRN). He had been instructed to deposit them in a safe."[205]

On 7 January 1972 the Orthodox celebrated services on the church square in temperatures of -20 degrees [Celsius]. Liturgies were held in these conditions until February 1972, when they were suspended. During

---

[202] Ibidem, Letter of Metropolitan Bazyli to Primate S. Wyszyński of 30 November 1971. The Polish Primate in a letter of January 1972 emphasized that the source of the conflict is taking over Greek Catholic propertyby the Orthodox Church. The primate stated that "he appealed (to the Metropolitan Stefan – from the author), to abandon the action of taking over the Catholic churches of Greek Cat. rite with violation of law". And further: "The violation of the rights of Catholics of the Greek Catholic Rite creates a sore situation. After all, Greek Catholics should enjoy legal protection in our common homeland", ibidem, Letter of Cardinal Stefan Wyszynski to the Metropolitan Bazyli of 2 January 1972

[203] Ibidem, Letter of Orthodox residents of Polany to Edward Gierek of 11 March 1972.

[204] Ibidem, Letter of Fr. J. Krysiak to UdSW of 11 December 1971. The Orthodox entered the church after finding the key to the padlock, which had been lost by the Catholics.

[205] Ibidem, Similar acts took place on 13 February 1972.

this period, Metropolitan Bazyli took up the issue of settlement of the conflict. In a letter to Cardinal Stefan Wyszyński he presented the origins and the course of the dispute over the church. He stressed that "in the spirit of ecumenism and love of neighbours" this issue should be solved rapidly for the good of both Churches and the faithful.[206]

The building was still occupied by Catholics who even organized special groups of believers armed with clubs that patrolled the area with dogs. To prevent a possible seizure of the church Fr. Pańczyszyn celebrated services every day in March and April 1972.[207]

In subsequent years the Orthodox church fought in court. Church services were celebrated outside the fence of the church square (among others by the priests Bazyli Janicki, Walenty Olesiuk, Andrzej Popławski, Michał Rydzanicz and Michał Żuk).

The Office for Religious Affairs also took a stance in the conflict in Polany. According to a memorandum drawn up in February 1972 the situation was "caused by the policy of Bishop Tokarczuk [...] who specifically engages clerics in this matter (priests Karabin, Szczepański, Wysoczański, Pańczyszyn). These priests artificially fuel national-religious antagonisms that have led to the apparent violation of government regulations and the state of legal ownership of the church [...], which is a parish of the Orthodox Church." The Office also blamed local authorities, who not only did not respond to the violation of legal provisions, but also deepened the conflict.[208]

According to the authorities the disputed building should be left in possession of the Orthodox parish and a prosecution should be launched, in order to reveal those responsible and bring them to criminal liability. It was also suggested to rebuke the local authorities that "under the circumstances their projects of sharing the building, or its handover to the Catholic side are not only wrong, but actually harmful politically. Moreover, they will result in the same conflict situations in the other 28

---

[206] Ibidem, Letter of Metropolitan Bazyli to Primate Stefan Wyszyński of 16 March 1972.

[207] "Wiadomości PAKP", 1972, no 2, p. 66. District Prosecutor's Office in Krosno on 29 May 1972 discontinued the investigation against the Roman Catholics due hacking into the church and its seizure, citing the absence of evidence, AAN, UdSW, The Department of Non-Catholic Faiths, sygn. 131/421, Letter of parish priests of Deanery Rzeszów to UdSW of 20 April 1973.

[208] Ibidem.

Orthodox places in the Rzeszów region."[209]

The situation influenced action addressed to state authorities. In March and May 1972, the Orthodox inhabitants of Polany addressed a petition to Edward Gierek and Piotr Jaroszewicz. They stated, among others, that "for many months in the village there has been a mess, lawlessness and law of the jungle as a result of undertakings by the Roman Catholic clergy who goaded the Catholic part of the population of our village and bringing supporting crusaders from neighboring villages, using axes and crowbars [...] took possession of our Orthodox church."[210]

On 9 April 1972, during Orthodox Easter, the faithful celebrated a solemn service in the rain.

A series of incidents directed against the Orthodox population started in May 1972. On 7 May Fr. Walenty Olesiuk was not let into the church square when he wanted to celebrate a liturgy.[211] In addition, while he was being beaten, the crowd shouted "kill the bastard, beggar, stinky priest, let's finish with him, break his legs so that he comes here no more." And: "remember, you lousy *pop* and you Orthodox pigs, that Orthodoxy is over [...] run out of here, otherwise you can say goodbye to your life."[212]

The situation in Polany was characterized by Fr. Bazyli Janicki (designated to celebrate worship on 14 May 1972): "The impression I got there, was not a Sunday spiritual mood, on the contrary, panic, anxiety, women with mouths and hands trembling from fear were busy on the farm, dressing up for the service, sighing about what will be there today, as if before an approaching storm." And further: "When I came with the faithful to the church, I noticed besiegers at the gate of the Orthodox Church, about 300 people brought by the priest Kazimierz Pańczyszyn on a crusade to Polany from neighboring villages, from Mszany, Krempna and Dukla [...] In the distance on a MO officer in plain clothes stood with several men from Polany and Myscowa [...] When I approached the gate and demanded we be let into the Orthodox Church to celebrate the lit-

[209] Ibidem, It was also suggested strengthening supervision "of the illegal activities of the Greek Catholic clergy, who inspired by Bishop Tokarczuk conducts offensive operations among the local population arousing nationalist sentiments".
[210] Ibidem, sygn. 131/421, Letter of Orthodox residents of Polany to Edward Gierek of 11 March 1972.
[211] Ibidem, Report of Fr. W. Olesiuk to the Vicarial Office in Sanok of 7 May 1972.
[212] Ibidem, Moreover, there were cries: "get out to Russia your Orthodoxy is there", "speed priests like dogs," or "run or I'll kill you like a hare".

urgy, they told me that this church was theirs, they have fixed everything with the authorities, and first and foremost, it was not an Orthodox but a Greek Catholic church. [...]at the request of the faithful I celebrated the service outside of the fence."[213]

These scandalous scenes also took place on 15 and 16 May 1972, when the faithful were offended with the words "the Ukrainians and Orthodox", and "an Orthodox villager was beaten" and Orthodox women insulted. "On 16 May some people threw stones at the houses of the Orthodox inhabitants."[214]

On 23 May 1972 the [Orthodox] dean of Rzeszów district Fr. Aleksander Dubec reminded the Office for Religious Affairs that twenty-four letters to the Office and other instances of the party and state had been issued in the matter of the parish in Polany in the period from 12 September 1971 until 19 May 1972. He demanded the dismissal of Fr. K. Pańczyszyn from Polany as "a public troublemaker and instigator of incidents and scandalous adventures, immediate withholding of construction work illegally continued by Catholics and re-sealing of the church until its return to its rightful user."[215]

During a Liturgy celebrated on 18 June 1972 by Fr. Andrzej Jakimiuk, the service was interupted by a person riding on a motorbike who ran around the gathered faithful "speeding at full volume, forcing the machine to make a terrible roar. Sudden laughter and cries of great joy were coming from a group of people standing at the gate. I finished the service in this noise, with screaming and derision directed at me."[216]

The Presidium of the Provincial National Council in Rzeszów also tried to solve the case of Polany. In June 1972 a meeting was held with Fr. Aleksander Dubec and Kazimierz Pańczyszyn. According to Fr. Dubec "the only possible solution to the conflict is to restore to Orthodox followers the use of the church [...]those who violated the rights of use and free religious practice for Orthodox believers, protected by the State, should

[213] Ibidem.
[214] Ibidem, Letter of the Orthodox Deanery of Rzeszów to the Office for Religious Affairs of 25 May 1972.
[215] Ibidem, Letter of Fr. A. Dubec to UdSW of 23 May 1972. In the letter the list of correspondence relating to parishes in Polany for the period from 12 September 1971 to 19 May 1972.
[216] Ibidem, Report of Fr. A. Jakimiuk to the Office of the Orthodox Deanery of District of Rzeszów of 22 June 1972.

be held to criminal liability and criminal and administrative liability."[217] Fr. Pańczyszyn suggested that the authorities are to blame for the situation because they had not issued permission before 1966 to transfer the church to Greek Catholics who "feel themselves the owners of the disputed church, because they or their fathers built it." At the same time, Fr. K. Pańczyszyn admitted that "the Roman Catholics' entrance to the church and taking it into possession was a wrongful act, but this fact is justified by the motives that were a source of the conflict."[218] There was not any acceptance of sharing the building, either.

In April 1973 parish priests of the Deanery of Rzeszów spoke about the case of Polany at the Deanery conference in Sanok. They stated, among others, that "the tragedy of the faithful in Polany is perceived by them and all our Church, as an act of rape and violence incompatible with the humanitarian principles of human ethics."[219]

Despite the ongoing conflict, Catholics began internal renovation of the church in Polany on 8 May 1973.

New hopes for resolving the situation for the faithful appeared with the election of Karol Wojtyła to the papacy. The parish council turned to John Paul II to intercede and help in resolving the dispute over the church. In a letter of May 1979, it was stated that: "In the atmosphere of a nationwide euphoria after the election of Your Holiness as Pope, as well as your announced and expected visit to Poland, also we- the members of a small community, the faithful of the Orthodox Parish in Polany, in the province of Krosno- accepted these facts with great animation and hope. Reading the speeches of Your Holiness in the press, we realized that a man who stands as the Highest Priest of the Roman Catholic Church who knows the conditions shaping the coexistence of fellow Christians in Poland and like no other from his predecessors, is able to understand the ills and often tragedies emerging against this background. Your Holiness' speech filled us with hope on matters concerning ecumenism, where we read from a distance of the great affairs of the Church we need to look at the small sometimes disputes that divide us. And so that's a little dispute, however, that for us is a great, unspeakable tragedy, we the

---

[217] Ibidem, Note from interviews with Fr. K. Pańczyszyn and Fr. A. Dubec on the elimination of the existing religious conflict, arising from using of the church in Polany of 3 July 1972.

[218] Ibidem.

[219] Ibidem, Letter of parish priests of Deanery Rzeszów to UdSW of 20 April 1973.

Orthodox faithful from Polany dare to turn to Your Holiness." And further: "The tragedy of ours is painfully felt by the whole Orthodox Church in Poland, as an act of rape and violence incompatible with the humanitarian principles of ethics in general and Christianity in particular, with the evangelical principle of love of neighbor. Currently, the world hears calls for respect for human dignity. Churches on the ecumenical path are also seeking ways of rapprochement. We know that Your Holiness is an ardent supporter of love, justice and respect for human rights, which was by Your Holiness emphatically underlined in a speech devoted to virtue and justice: *there can be no love without justice [...]. If justice is undermined, even love is in danger.* Strongly buoyed by that quoted above, we believe that Your Holiness [...] in the name of Christian justice, will come to our aid and [...] will improve our difficult situation and will provide us with the access to a house of worship rebuilt by us to run our religious practices, at least in form of sharing. And we, on our part, except for the dogmatic as well as jurisdictional differences, after very fair, in which we do not doubt, solution of our so painful problem, we will pray to the Only One, glorified by all of us Christians, God in the Trinity for happy and prolific on the path of ecumenism pontificate of Your Holiness. Today we send to Your Holiness a heartfelt God bless you."[220]. This approach also did not bring a solution.

The conflict in Polany and the lack of a solution to it by the Polish authorities became known outside the country. Besides the Vatican, the Orthodox intervened in this matter, among others, with the Patriarch of Constantinople and Patriarch of Moscow. Even at the "highest level" a compromise that would end these tragic events was not reached.

They also turned to Polish Primate Cardinal Stefan Wyszyński to intervene. In a letter of March 1980, it was stated that "the fact of taking away the church from us by the followers of your Church has become an unspeakable tragedy for us. We did not build the Tower of Babel. We rebuilt the temple of the Lord. We carried this huge, for us, weight with joy in our hearts. We did not even think that we would be punished for that, very severely punished, and our judges would be the followers of the same Christ the Lord. We realize that the ruins of the church were once a Uniate building. Another thing is that our fathers built it, and even

---

[220] Ibidem, sygn. 132/215, Letter of the Orthodox Parish Council in Polany to John Paul II of 4 May 1979.

some of us who remember those times are still living. And although we returned to the Orthodox Church [...] we were not deprived of all rights in relation to the church [building.] It is known that we have always been associated with the Byzantine culture. There would not be so great regret in us, if, when the ruins of the winter represented a barrel of snow and in summer the young crown of the trees were green, someone then took care of them. It was not like that. We did this ourselves. It is not our sin that the competent authorities of our country gave us the ruins, when we asked for them [...]. We live still with the small flame of faith in the fact that love in the Gospel of Christ the Lord will dwell in the hearts of our warring communities. We humbly ask Your Eminence to make the harm be redressed. In the current environment it is easier for the Roman Catholic Church to build a huge building than for us few, nailed, and despised, a tiny chapel."[221] These efforts also did not bring any positive results.

On 29 December 1982, the District Court of Krosno issued a decision on sharing the church in Polany. However, Fr. K. Pańczyszyn with his faithful did not comply with the court order.

The Secretariat of the Polish Episcopate also tried to solve this issue. The suspension of court proceedings was suggested, and then making a concerted effort "to build a chapel for the Orthodox believers of the municipality; the Roman Catholic parish would help materially in the construction, bearing part of the cost, the amount of which would correspond to the value of the expenditure incurred for the renovation earlier by the followers of the Orthodox Church. The Bishops' Curia in Przemyśl would supervise the proper execution of the agreement by the Roman Catholic parish. Indeed, it is undisputed that at present the Orthodox community in Polany is very tiny."[222]. The above proposal was also not accepted. According to the "local Catholics, there will not be Orthodoxy in Polany anymore".

The situation that occurred in Polany also influenced the position of the Orthodox in other regions of Lemkovyna. Among other things, the faithful in Rozdziele remarked on the initiative of building their own

---

[221] Ibidem, Letter of the Orthodox Parish Council in Polany to the Polish Primate Fr. Cardinal Stefan Wyszyński of 12 March 1980. The issue was again raised in the letters of 1 February 1981 and to the Polish Primate Fr. Cardinal Józef Glemp of 23 November 1985.

[222] Ibidem, Letter of Archbishop Bronisław Dąbrowski to Metropolitan Bazyli of 19 January 1983.

temple: "To build? That is what the people from Polany did, rebuilt the church, which had been abandoned for 22 years. They toiled building like stupid donkeys; the Roman Catholics walked in and laughed at them, saying, 'Do it, do it, we will take it anyway.'"[223] According to the Orthodox Archbishop Adam the taking of the church in Polany would "usher in a series of this type of lawlessness. The Orthodox churches in Zapałów, Pielgrzymka and Kłokowice were to share the fate of Polany. This was to be the first step in destroying Orthodoxy in this area."[224]

"The Conflict of Polany" would not be resolved by the end of communist rule in Poland. The Orthodox Christians celebrated worship "under the sky" for many years. On 23 May 1989 the square where there was a church with a parish house, the bell tower and cemetery, became the property of the Catholic parish. The church has been shared by the Roman Catholic parish and the Greek Catholic faithful since 1992.

The Orthodox faithful still celebrated their devotion at the wall of the church. In 1991 Fr. Bazyli Gałczyk (son of Jan Gałczyk), in his sermon to the faithful after the liturgy, said: "Christians dealt this fate to Christians." The memorial service after the death of Jan Gałczyk in 1988 was characteristic of the whole situation, the ongoing years-long dispute: it took place at the church wall. Bishop Adam, assessing events in Polany, stated that "was an example of cooperation between the government, the [communist] party and the Roman Catholic Church against the Orthodox Church. People in Polany knew that this was a Rusyn Orthodox church. The Orthodox refurbished it. Then the church was taken from them. None of those who had violated the law of possession was punished even a bit." According to Fr. Leszek Moryl (in 1995, the Roman Catholic priest in Polany): "Here all are harmed: Orthodox, Greek Catholics, and Roman Catholics."[225]

The Orthodox parish in Polany with its subsidiary in Zyndranowa was closed in 2003.[226] In the lovely words of J. L. Sobolewski, "A lot of time will pass before time heals the painful wounds caused by this quite unnecessary conflict, the result of an overgrowth of purely human ambi-

[223] Ibidem, sygn. 131/423, Letter of Fr. A. Dubec to Metropolitan Bazyli of 4 March 1972.
[224] A. Radziukiewicz, Weź krzyż i idź za mną, "Przegląd Prawosławny", 2003, no 3, p. 5.
[225] M. Bołtryk, op. cit., p. 87.
[226] "Wiadomości PAKP", 2003, no 6, p. 18, see also "Przegląd Prawosławny", 2006, no 10, p. 4.

tions on the common message of all religions which commands love, peace, tolerance ..."[227]

∗∗∗

The nearly thirty-year struggle of Orthodox believers to establish a parish in Rozdziele and the long-standing conflict over the opportunity to celebrate Orthodox religious services in Polany were part of a policy of state authorities towards the Polish Autocephalous Orthodox Church. By blocking the erection of new parishes and stirring up disputes among believers, the state authorities tried to influence the actions and behavior (social and political) of church authorities. They used the well-known method of *divide and rule*, which provided great opportunities to shape the religious life of religious minorities in postwar Poland.[228]

---

[227] J. L. Sobolewski, op. cit.
[228] See more: R. Michalak, Polityka wyznaniowa państwa polskiego..., p. 75-112.

Church in Brunary, Grybow County

CHAPTER 4

The non-religious role of the Orthodox Church in the life of Lemkos after 1947

The resettlement operations in the years 1944-1947 led to the disorganization of the interwar administrative structures of the Orthodox Church in Lemkovyna. The method of carrying out evictions, the accompanying repressions and the dispersion of the faithful contributed to a decrease in the number of believers, as well as religious conversions and secularization. In the material sphere, the Church lost most of its property and many of its often-historic houses of worship were destroyed. At the same time the clergy and the faithful were forced to build new parish structures in the extreme conditions of new areas of settlement.[229]

After 1947 the Orthodox Church carried out cultural and community-building functions among Lemkos in the western territories and, as a result of partial returns, in Lemkovyna after 1956. The first Orthodox institutions created in the western territories were erected at the end of 1947 (e.g. Buczyna, Jawor, Jelenia Góra, Studzionki and Zimna Woda). Lemkos co-created parishes, among others, in Legnica, Lipiny, Kożuchów, Przemków, Wrocław, Rudna, Lubin, Leszno Górne, Ługi, Brzoza, Samborz, Malczyce, Michałów, Torzym, Głogów and Zielona Góra. Administratively they were a part of the Diocese of Wrocław and Szczecin, formed in September 1951.[230]

The integrative and cultural role of the Orthodox Church was huge in the initial period. Orthodox parishes with newly established parish councils and church choirs became the first forms of organized activity

---

[229] G. Kuprianowicz, Akcja „Wisła" a Kościół prawosławny..., p. 153, 172.
[230] To 1951 the administrative structure of the Orthodox Church in the western territories was based on Administration for Orthodox Parishes in the Recovered Territories and the Diocese of Recovered Territories established on 15 July 1946. In 1948 deaneries of Wrocław and Szczecin were included in the newly erected diocese of Łódź and Wrocław. Most of the Lemko people lived in the deaneries of Wrocław and Zielona Góra, see more: P. Gerent, Prawosławie na Dolnym Śląsku w latach 1945-1989, Toruń 2007; S. Dudra, Cerkiew w diasporze. Z dziejów prawosławnej diecezji wrocławsko-szczecińskiej, Poznań 2009.

among the Lemko population after the resettlement. They were primarily focused on maintenance and activity.

Orthodox parishes were also the site of the first attempts at organized cultural activities among the displaced. The front yard of the church building became a meeting place for the faithful. It fulfilled an important social and organizational function. It was just before and after the liturgy that they could talk about the possibility of return to their homes, or exchange information about missing family members and the conditions of life in the new land. They discussed the future. They also made the first plans for building religious life in a new place of residence. Later, they also commented on important socio-political and economic events taking place in the country. For most forcibly displaced Lemkos the Orthodox Church took on special significance. It became a mainstay of identity, primarily religious, but also cultural and ethnic.

As a result of their resettlement, the cultural life of Lemkos was drastically inhibited. Rituals and customs disappeared, often due to the hostile attitude of Polish society. "Merged into places with a predominance of Polish settlers, they eliminated those elements of their traditional culture that exposed them to the ridicule of their new neighbors. At the same time, they acquired local cultural patterns."[231] Undoubtedly, folk tradition passed on in the form of songs, tales, customs, holidays linked very strongly with the Orthodox Church made it possible to preserve their autonomy and identity.

In the first period the cultural life of the Lemko people went on primarily in the closed family circle. Singing songs of "those brought from the mountains" would keep up spirits. At the same time all kinds of religious celebrations (weddings, baptisms and even funerals) became a social occasion for joint "experiencing their own past" and an attempt to build and develop their own culture, often adapted to the new reality in the new surroundings.

Parish church committees played an important integrating role in the initial period of existence of the Orthodox. Together with clerics, they organized religious life in villages. Often called "committees of construction" they restored [former German] houses of worship to working condition (most sacred buildings were in ruins and required significant repairs.)

---

[231] Cit. after D. Blin-Olbert, Rok obrzędowy u Łemków, [in:] Łemkowie w historii i kulturze Karpat, ed. J. Czajkowski, Sanok 1994, vol. 2, p. 313.

Organization of places of worship was an important element in the functioning of the Church. In many cases, the first church services were celebrated in private homes, or hospital and cemetery chapels. Entire parish communities were involved in renovations of churches [ruined in the war.] Due to the lack of state aid the faithful themselves incurred the costs. In special cases (costly overhauls, a small number of the faithful in the parish) metropolitan and diocesan collections were carried out. Measures were also undertaken to equip them properly (with icons and liturgical books). Objects necessary to celebrate Orthodox worship came from areas where the Orthodox Lemko population had been displaced from, e.g. those used in Ługi (Zielona Góra deanery) came from the church in Regetów (Gorlice county). Also, icons adorning the walls of church buildings often came from the churches in Lemkovyna. They were for many years the only elements connecting Lemkos with their "little homeland."

In most cases, the creation of Orthodox parishes was a grassroots initiative by Lemko people. The formation of the Orthodox church in Torzym was described by a newcomer from Florynka: "The Lemko families settled here were a small community. We were about 85 people [...]. Greek Catholics somehow one by one, then with gathering force, went to the Roman Catholic Church. The Orthodox had more resistance. Banding together, they decided that in the former German cemetery in Torzym there was a small chapel which could be done over on the model of an Orthodox chapel [...]. It was repaired quickly. They brought the icons carried from Florynka to the chapel. This is how a house of worship was created in the likeness of a small Orthodox church."[232]

The first liturgies were a big event for the displaced Orthodox community. "A lot of people gathered, because the news went through the area that Orthodox divine service will be in Torzym. People were waiting long before the start of the service. They came, however they could, even from a distance of forty kilometers (from Glisno, Wielowieś, Łagów and many others.) Divine service began, and with it sobbing and crying. [...] People prayed and sang in their own way, as in the past on their land in Florynka [...]. Thus began the re-integration, or re-building of a community in exile."[233]

---

[232] J. Zwoliński, Rapsodia dla Łemków, Koszalin 1994, p. 49.
[233] Ibidem, p. 51.

Pastoral work was an important integrative and culture-building element of the Orthodox Church among young Lemko people. Until 1989, it focused mainly on catechesis. Orthodox religious education was especially important in the western territories. It became an important factor in preserving Lemkos' identity. Often carried out in unfavorable external conditions, it was a carrier of identity and an element of building a new life among the youngest generation of the Orthodox community.

The significant dispersion of the Lemko people, due to the nature and principles of "Operation Vistula" ruled out, in practice, the teaching of religion at schools. Also, church authorities were negative about the teaching of religion at schools in the diaspora, due to the extremely low level of interfaith tolerance.[234] An important factor was also the reluctance of parents and the children themselves to participate in organized catechism classes at school (insults, threats, cases of fisticuffs were not unusual phenomena.) For these reasons, the teaching of religion was carried out at parish sites and, especially in the first years after resettlement, in private homes, then, in the years 1956-1960 partly at schools. [Note that even in communist times, religion could be taught in public schools.] The lessons were taught by priests caring for a given parish. Since 1961, catechesis was carried out and flourished in catechetical centers located in parishes. In many cases, the return of religion to centers in parishes caused children and young people to have a greater interest in learning it. This was due to various factors, among which the main one was lower pressure exerted by their surroundings. Because of transportation difficulties, classes were often held after Sunday liturgies, which facilitated children's taking part in them. During religious education children could freely, outside the home, communicate in their own language. Also, they often received extra lessons on the complex history of their ancestors.

Since 1991, children and Lemko youth have had religious education in state schools. A series of catechetical meetings has also been held in most Orthodox parishes. In addition to religious issues important social issues (including the problems of drug addiction, alcoholism, and secularization) have also been discussed.

A transformational turning point in Orthodox youth participation was the creation of the Brotherhood of Orthodox Youth (BMP) in 1981.[235] In

---

[234] K. Urban, Kościół prawosławny w Polsce 1945-1970 (rys historyczny)..., p. 282.
[235] First it was called the Theologians Circle of Orthodox Theological Schools, Laity and

1982, the first charter of the organization was approved. Its main activities were recruiting youth involvement and organizing events (including pilgrimages to the monastery at the Holy Mountain of Grabarka and to the monastery of St. Onufry in Jabłeczna), summer and winter camps, and establishing international contacts. In the first half of the 1980s the organization gained a presence in the western territories (diocese of Wrocław and Szczecin). This was the culmination of vigorous activity, started in the late 1960s, by Dr. Jan Anchimiuk, later diocesean Bishop Jeremiasz (Anchimiuk). In 1984, a Diocesan Youth Council (the equivalent of the Brotherhood in the diocesan structure) began its work. Its task was to inspire and coordinate the work of the Brotherhood circles operating in its territory. It was also involved actively in organizing pilgrimages, summer and winter camps for children and youth. In 1987 there were three circles of the Brotherhood on the territory of the diocese. One of their activities was to organize retreats and pastoral conferences for youth.[236]

As a result of the partial liberalization in government policy towards national minorities after 1956, the gradual revival of Orthodox religious life in Lemkovyna began. This was due to the fact that some of the displaced people were able to return to their homeland. Returning Lemkos started to campaign for restoration of the parishes or creation of new ones.[237] In 1956 worship began in Bartne and Wysowa. In 1957 a parish was established in Bodaki, and since 1958 services have been celebrated in Blechnarka and Hańczowa. Then, pastoral posts were erected in, among others, Bielanka, Gładyszów, Zagórz, Pielgrzymka, Morochów,

---

Secular Youth. In 1982 the first charter was adopted. The guardian on behalf of St. Council of Bishops was Bishop Sawa, and the first president was elected Eugeniusz Czykwin. Under the Act on the Relation of the State to PAKP of 4 July 1991, The Brotherhood gained legal status in the church and found themselves in the organizational structure, about the genesis and activity of BMP see: J. Charkiewicz, Bractwo Młodzieży Prawosławnej w Polsce, Białystok 1995.

[236] Such a conference was held in 1985 in Szczecin. The program included, among others, the outline of the history of the Orthodox Church in Poland, the decor of the Church and its importance, and the establishment and significance of Christmas on the basis of icons, Archives of Orthodox Diocese of Wrocław and Szczecin (APDWSz), The report from the retreat-pastoral youth conference held in Szczecin on 20-22 December 1985.

[237] Such activities were conducted in the first half of the 50s. Among others in 1953 Fr. Jan Lewiarz attempted to run a parish in Bartne, but that ended in failure. Metropolitan Makary returned to the issue in early 1955. However, only in 1956 they managed to run the parish, see: P. Gerent, Proces powstawania parafii prawosławnych na Podkarpaciu po 1956 roku, "Antyfon", 2006, no 1, p. 11.

Leszczyny, Zdynia Konieczna, Regetów, Zyndranowa, Rozdziele, Gorlice and Kwiatoń. In 1983, the Lemko Orthodox parishes were incorporated into the newly created Diocese of Przemyśl-Nowy Sącz[238].

Joint work on the reconstruction and the restoration of buildings re-integrated local communities. The first services "in the mountains" were an important event in the life of Lemkos. The Orthodox Church again became an important culture-creating element. Among others, its organized activity led to the reconstruction of parish cemeteries and the recovery of valuable and historic icons and church accessories.

Until 1989, the Orthodox Church, despite the limited ability to act under the policy of state authorities, was an important factor integrating Lemkos and at the same time an important means of creating culture within the history of this community. An Orthodox church was one of the few places where besides the liturgy, they could hear the sermon and singing in "their language" [*po-nashomu*, "in our way"]. In churches and presbyteries, they sang traditional Orthodox Christmas carols. This enabled them to survive the difficult period in which government policy was not conducive to the development of national minorities.

The role of the Orthodox Church in culture and integration after 1989

As a result of the democratic changes taking place in Poland after 1989 the Orthodox Church began a new period in its activities. In addition to integrating the community, due to emerging opportunities, it could fulfill a wider range of the creation of culture. This concerned both the western territories and Lemkovyna. Church buildings became the site of numerous speeches and lectures devoted to the history and culture of Lemkos and Lemkovyna. They focused mainly on those elements that, because of the political situation and censorship, were outside the mainstream during the postwar period (including UPA activity in Lemkovyna, causes of "Operation Vistula", and the camp in Jaworzno.)

---

[238] On 7 September 1951 after the reorganization of diocesan structure by Metropolitan Makary the provinces of Kraków and Rzeszów were in the Diocese of Łódź and Poznań. As part of the adjustments made on 30 April 1958 by the Council of Bishops of PAKP the Rzeszów province was incorporated into the Diocese of Warszawa and Bielsk.

In the western territories the activity of The Brotherhood of Orthodox Youth of the Diocese of Wrocław and Szczecin, which Lemko youth
formed the backbone of, intensified. Among others, there were new
ecumenical and ecological programs, courses in foreign languages and
learning to write [paint] icons, and retreat activities.[239] Lemko youth
actively participated in the pilgrimage movement. They were also involved
in church charity.[240]

In January 1990 the Orthodox Association of Saints Piotr and Paweł
[Saints Peter and Paul] at Wrocław Cathedral parish began its activity.
Within the framework of the Association, sections were established
dedicated to science and education, catechesis, charity, international
cooperation and publishing. There are also branch offices working in
Szczecin and Lubin. The organization's activity is focused on educational
issues (symposia in Cieplice, Thursday meetings in Wrocław), as well as
charitable and youth work (organization of summer and winter camps).
Furthermore, it is the organizer of "Eve" for singles, pilgrimages (domestic
and foreign) and ecumenical meetings. Holiday stays for pensioners held
at a resort in Cieplice have become very popular.[241]

The Orthodox Church Nursing Home of St. Stefan in Cieplice has held
a broad range of culture-creating activities since 1991.[242] It directs these
activities primarily towards children and young people. Besides camps
during winter and summer holidays, its program includes Orthodox
religious education, church singing lessons, games and competitions
helping to understand the history and traditions of the Orthodox Church.
Foreign language courses have also been organized there by, among
others, representatives of the World Student Christian Federation. The

---

[239] J. Charkiewicz, op. cit., p. 33; O. Hajduczenia, Wychowawcze oddziaływanie
wybranych form działalności Bractwa Młodzieży Prawosławnej, Białystok 1990, p.
46.

[240] Charitable activities were carried out within the framework of Orthodox Charity
Center "Eleos" of Diocese of Wrocław and Szczecin founded in 2001.

[241] See more: A. Rydzanicz, Stowarzyszenie ma przyszłość, "Przegląd Prawosławny",
2011, no 1, p. 26-28.

[242] The idea of its construction was to create a house that was supposed to be a
refuge for the elderly (both clergy and laity) who tied their lives with the Orthodox
Church. The immediate cause of endeavor for construction of the facility was the
necessity to move the retired Fr. Konstanty Bajko, a priest dedicated to the life
of the Church (including prisoner labor camps in the Soviet Union). Throughout
the diocese there was no place where he could settle down after a long period of
pastoral work. Work on its creation was carried out since the mid 80s of the last
century, see: 20 lat służby arcypasterskiej, "Wiadomości PAKP", 2003, no 9.

funds were provided by the World Council of Churches and the Orthodox Youth Federation "Syndesmos."[243] Many initiatives were also directed to adults. Conferences dedicated to the history of Christianity and discussion meetings on current life problems of the Church in Poland became an indelible part of the calendar of activities of the resort.

In the last two decades the Nursing Home in Cieplice has been the location of, among others, conferences of representatives of the clergy and laity of the diocese of Wrocław and Szczecin, conventions of diocesan brotherhoods of the Brotherhood of Orthodox Youth and theological courses for members of parish councils. The resort has also hosted foreign delegations (including delegates of the Orthodox Church in Kenya, children and youth from Ukraine and Belarus in relation to the "Chernobyl" disaster.) The Singing School of the Orthodox Diocese of Wrocław and Szczecin also has its headquarters in the resort. Cieplice has become an institution that meets an important role, both religious as well as cultural and educational in the life of the faithful of the diocese of Wrocław and Szczecin and the entire Orthodox community in Poland. It has also become an important center for integrating the diaspora Orthodox community into western Poland.[244]

After 1989, many Orthodox parishes have also joined activities of a cultural nature. In November 1992, at the initiative of Fr. Artur Graban (parish priest in Ługi and Brzoza, Szczecin Deanery) the Association of Lovers of Lemko Culture in Ługi was formed. Its aim is to nurture, develop and disseminate Lemko spiritual and material culture, bring together Lemko people regardless of religious views and beliefs, and shape youth social and cultural elites. These objectives are implemented by organizing cultural and educational activities (performances and ensemble meetings, concerts, theater performances, lectures, seminars), conducting classes to give children and youth knowledge of the history and culture of the Lemko people, the creation of artistic groups and centers to promote Lemko culture and art (clubs, libraries, museum and ethnographic chambers) and issuing their own magazines and books.[245]

---

[243] Information about summer and winter camps in Cieplice see: "Przegląd Prawosławny", years 1992-2015.

[244] See more: „Roczniki Prawosławnej Diecezji Wrocławsko-Szczecińskiej", years 2004-2015.

[245] The charter of the Association of Lovers of Lemko Culture in Ługi (in author's archives).

A music band "Chwylyna" works at the Association, and an outdoor event "Lemko Watra in Ługi" has also been organized.[246] In 2003, the Association received its own premises in an old, disused water tower, named the "Lemko Tower" [Lemko Tower has appeared on Youtube]. This building was renovated by mid-2006, while meetings, exhibitions and shows of bands and choirs took place there. The Association also conducts ensembles,[247] publishing activity,[248] and organizes several cultural and educational projects, including trips for children and youth to Lemkovyna "encounters" with contemporary Lemko culture; "Autumn in the Carpathians"– preparation and presentation, in the Lemko language, of a play by Piotr Trochanowski; "Summer School of Lemko culture"– a project carried out in collaboration with the *Society Lemkiwszczyna and Young Lemkiwszczyna* from Ukraine; "From Nikifor to Warhol"– creative and educational workshops, an icon-writing school, photography, theater and music workshops; "Rus' twilight"– poetry readings and Lemko songs; and "Our Book"– a project to collect and compile the memoirs of Lemko residents of Strzelce-Drezdenko district.[249] In 2011, Fr. Artur Graban was awarded a Silver Cross of Merit by President Bronisław Komorowski for his contribution to the protection, preservation and development of cultural identity of Lemkos.

On a smaller scale, cultural activities are also conducted in other centers. Among others, the Orthodox parish of the Holy Trinity in Lubin hosts regular workshops of writing [painting] icons for children and adolescents. They are led by iconographer Jan Grigoruk, a graduate of the School of Iconography in Bielsk Podlaski. Moreover, a division of

---

[246] The Folk Music Ensemble "Chwylyna" was set up in 1989, and the first meeting of "Watra" participants took place in 1991.

[247] In 2004 the folk group „Lemko Tower" was created on the initiative of Fr. A. Graban. Its members were students of primary and junior high school. It was run by Oleh Smolej. In 2005 O. Smolej created the rock group "JARRO" which presented the Lemko music.

[248] Among others they issued: Z łemkowskiej skrzyni. Opowieści z Ługów i okolic, part. 1, Strzelce Krajeńskie 2003; Opowieści z Brzozy i okolic, part. 2, Strzelce Krajeńskie 2004; W. Graban, Znaleźć równowagę duszy, Strzelce Krajeńskie 2004; A. Dudra, S. Dudra, Prawosławny dekanat zielonogórski, Strzelce Krajeńskie 2004; A. Dudra, S. Dudra, Prawosławny dekanat lubiński, Strzelce Krajeńskie-Krynica Zdrój 2005; Ikony cerkwi prawosławnej w Brzozie, Strzelce Krajeńskie 2005.

[249] A. Graban, Działalność społeczno-kulturalna Łemków na terenie powiatu strzelecko-drezdeneckiego, [in:] Łemkowie. Historia i kultura. Sesja naukowa Szreniawa 30 czerwca-1 lipca 2007, Szreniawa 2007, p. 109-111; B. Horbal, Lemko Studies: A Handbook, New York 2010, p. 476.

the Association of Orthodox Sts. Piotr and Paweł [Saints Peter and Paul] in Lubin is also the organizer of the outdoor community event "Lemko welcome summer". Concerts, recitation competitions, and sporting events, among others, take place during its course. Workshops devoted to the writing [painting] of Easter eggs are very popular. They relate to the tradition of Lemkovyna in many ways.

In addition, the parish at Świdnica organized workshops for painting icons, while those at Rudna and Ługi put on the traditional Christmas play, and St. Nicholas and Christmas meetings have been popular at Legnica, Przemków, Szczecin, and Zielona Góra. Many parishes have periodic lectures on the history and culture of the Orthodox Church and the role of Lemkos in the life of the Church. Teaching of the Lemko language is also held by, among others, Orthodox clergy in Brzoza, Lubin, Ługi and Zielona Góra.

The Orthodox Sports Organization of the Republic of Poland, established in 1994, plays an important role in keeping Lemko Orthodox youth active and building community among them.[250] The development of competitive sports, recreation, tourism and the organization of youth camps were outlined as its main tasks. In 1995 its structures were formed in the Diocese of Wrocław and Szczecin.[251] In addition to organizing many sports and recreation events, since 1999 it has been co-organizer, together with the Lutheran Sports Organization, of an "ecumenical rally" on the Sokołowsko-Wałbrzych route. Its participants are involved in numerous church services and visit the houses of worship of various faiths on the way. Tourist Hiking Tours are also very popular (including Sokołowsko-Rock City in the Czech Republic) and a regular sports and recreation event for children and youth "All together in sport and recreation" is organized during the Lemko "Watra" in Michałów.

The political changes in Poland after 1989 also contributed to a recovery in activity of Lemkos in the Diocese of Przemyśl-Nowy Sącz. Since

[250] Its creator was Jan Roman Braun (Director of the Centre of Eastern Martial Arts in Warsaw). The Genesis The Orthodox Sports Organization of the Republic of Poland is associated with the Sports Committee, set up by Piotr Nazaruk in Bielsk Podlaski. The founding congress of the organization took place in the parish house at Wola in Warsaw on 26 November 1994. The president of The Orthodox Sports Organization of the Republic of Poland became Fr. M. Lenczewski, the organizational vice president J. R. Braun, see: Duch sportu, "Przegląd Prawosławny", 1995, no 1.
[251] The first president was Andrzej Bołkowski, Fr. Lubomir Worhacz (the parish priest in Legnica) has been the president since 1999.

1992 the Brotherhood of Orthodox Youth of the Diocese of Przemyśl-Nowy Sącz has been functioning. It has, among others, organized cycling tours on the routes of "The Destroyed churches" and "St. Maksym Gorlicki" and pilgrimages to the Holy Mount Jawor and to the monastery in Ujkowice. It has also been actively involved in actions to organize summer and winter camps for children and youth.[252]

Similarly, as in the case of the western territories, the Diocesan Sports Organization created in 1996 enjoys great popularity among the youngest Lemkos. It organizes diocesan events. In 2001 the "Karpaty" Orthodox Student Sports Club was founded at the parish in Gładyszów. Fr. Arkadiusz Barańczuk serves as the president. According to its by-laws the club is to specialize in several sports and tourism disciplines (table tennis, chess and horseback riding.[253]

In 2000, the "Elpis" Diocesan Centre of Orthodox Culture was created in Gorlice.[254] Its mission is to spread Orthodox culture through religious and educational training. As part of the center there are specialized departments: Department of Catechism, the Diocesan Library, the Diocesan Museum and the Carpathian Archives. They also continue publishing activity. The editors of the quarterly "Antyfon" and "Almanach Diecezjalny" are located in its headquarters.[255] Lemko issues are presented on their pages. The periodic National Competition for Recitation of Lemko Poetry is also carried out in the Orthodox Cultural Center building in Gorlice. The participants are young Lemkos, students of primary and secondary schools, representing the institutions and teaching sites of the Lemko language from all of Poland.

The "Elpis" Diocesan Centre of Orthodox Culture in Gorlice was also the initiator of inventory and restoration of Lemko cemeteries. The first works started in 2001 in the community of Sękowa in Gorlice county within the project "Memory stronger than death". Among others, cemeteries in the now non-existent villages of Radocyna, Długie, Lipna and Hyrowa were renewed. The activity is ecumenical; young people of different faiths and nationalities (Poles, Lemkos, Slovaks, and Ukrainians)

---

[252] About the forms of Brotherhood activities see: the quarterly "Antyfon".
[253] See: "Antyfon", 2001, no 4, p. 45.
[254] APDWSz, The decree of Archbishop Adam of Przemyśl and Nowy Sącz from 11 September 2000, the care of the Centre has been entrusted to Fr. Roman Dubec.
[255] The first issue of "Antyfon" (no 1-2) was in 1997, and the first volume of "Almanach Diecezjalny" in 2005.

were involved in the work. These are, among others, cleaning crosses, straightening out inclined monuments, tacking together broken and cracked parts and general restoration work. There are plans to restore further post-Lemko cemeteries and roadside crosses.[256]

The major secular Lemko organizations, Lemko Association (formed in 1989) and Union of Lemkos (1990), also started collaboration with Orthodox parishes. An important element of integration is the Lemko "Watras" which are held in Zdynia, Michałów and Ługi. Although they are secular initiatives, they receive the support of the Orthodox hierarchy and clergy who actively participate in these "festival(s) of Lemko culture". "Watras" [bonfires] meet important cultural and cognitive needs: the popularization of culture and art, numerous contests on history of Lemkos and Lemkovyna. Kermeshes [festive gatherings] must also be placed in a similar context– generally held on the patron saint's day of a Lemko Orthodox church, they refer to the traditional celebration of patronal feasts in interwar Lemkovyna, and have religious, cultural and ecumenical dimensions. During these celebrations, besides their liturgical part, many cultural events are held: performances of Lemko ensembles, exhibitions of photography and painting, presentation of regional products.

An important cultural and at the same time unifying role is played the aforementioned cult of St. Maksym Gorlicki among the Orthodox Lemkos, both in the western territories and in Lemkovyna. The priest-martyr Maksym Gorlicki is today a symbol of martyrdom of Lemkos, ongoing with their traditions and the Orthodox faith of their forefathers. One of the tangible manifestations of the cult among Lemkos are icons with his image found in many churches Lemko and temples dedicated to him. The parish feasts are celebrated with due ceremony on the day of the patron [in accordance of the church calendar.]

In 2007, the Orthodox Church was the organizer of nationwide commemorations of the 60th anniversary of the "Operation Vistula". The main commemoration was held in the parish of Przemków (province Dolny Śląsk). This parish had symbolic importance because it was created by people displaced from Lemkovyna (among others from Bieliczna,

---

[256] The result of the initiative was also publishing Inwentaryzacja łemkowskich cmentarzy w nieistniejących wsiach na terenie gminy Sękowa. part 1. Banica, Długie, Lipna (stan na 31.10.2002)", ed. R. Dubec, Gorlice 2003, more about the project "Memory stronger than death" see the quarterly "Antyfon" years 2001-2014.

Florynka, Piorunka, Stawisza), and the town itself, due to the significant concentration of this community was called "the Lemko capital."

In conclusion, the Orthodox Church has played an important role in integration and cultural creation among Lemkos. As Michał Łesiów emphasized, writing about the culture-creating role of the Ukrainian Greek Catholic Church: religion is an important part of the culture of the nation. The form and content of religion comes often into the national consciousness; it contributes greatly to the development of national culture, or at least should support this development.[257]

In the case of Lemkos this issue was complex. This is because they belong to two churches: the Greek Catholic and the Orthodox. In addition, there are differences of identity: some Lemkos identify with the Ukrainian nation, while others reject Ukrainian national consciousness. The Orthodox Church asserts the primacy of faith in relation to the diversity of nationalities and national situation of believers, and does not differentiate them ethnically.[258] Although it has not become a base for all social or political minorities who belong to it (including Belarusians and Ukrainians) it has played an important role in the culture-creating and integration process of Lemkos. It has played a positive role in the development of their language and cultural identity. In many churches sermons were (and still are) given in the Lemko language. They are also a place where you can buy newspapers and publications devoted to this group of people.

---

[257] M. Łesiów, Rola kulturotwórcza Ukraińskiej Cerkwi Greckokatolickiej, Lublin 2001, p. 11.
[258] E. Czykwin, Między ziemią a wiarą, "Przegląd Prawosławny", 1995, no 7

Church in Konieczna

CHAPTER 5

The Lemko path to nationhood

In the Polish Census of 2010, national or ethnic origin was defined as "a declarative (based on a subjective feeling), individual feature of every human being, expressing his emotional, cultural or genealogical relationship with a particular nation or ethnic community."[259] The modern definition of a nation should take into account contemporary criteria for identification; in this the most important statement is the question of nationality: I am who I feel. These conditions also apply to the Lemko population.

Lemkos "became" a nation in a long historical process, which was initiated in the sixteenth century with the birth of Lemko literature. The next literary development came in the second half of the nineteenth century. Language and literature, alongside history and culture, became the main national-creative factors. The Lemko population, until the outbreak of World War II, lived in the area called Lemkivshchyna by their Polish neighbors, while Lemkos used the name Lemkovyna. It covered areas of the Central Carpathians, and the population, in a compact mass, inhabited areas of the Beskid Niski and Sądecki [mountains/hills]. The same as Boykos and, further to the east, Hutsuls, they were a community possessing its own, separate general sense of Lemko nationality created through centuries of culture. These processes were interrupted by the events of the years 1944-1947. The events associated with "Operation Vistula" were particularly tragic. Paradoxically, because of these events' threat to identity, they caused an acceleration of a national revival among the Lemkos [in the late 20th and early 21st centuries].

A process beginning in the nineteenth century had significant influence on creation of the Lemko national identity. This process was associated with the development of several movements. The Russophile one preached the idea of a unification of all of the nations of Rus' under the rule of the Tsar, at the same time promoting Orthodoxy. The *Starorus'* or Old Rus' one emphasized the historical, linguistic and cultural separateness of Lemko-Rusyns. Activists of both these currents opposed all

---

[259] www.spis.gov.pl [10 March 2012].

attempts at imposing a Ukrainian national consciousness [on Lemkos]. A manifestation of this type of activity was, among others, the establishment of the socio-cultural organization "Lemko-Soyuz" [Lemko Association] in 1933, whose main aim was primarily to defend against Ukrainization.[260]

The Lemko population had a strong tendency to express its own identity and nationality. They had an outstanding sense of ethnic separateness– though generally a passive one, as stated in the mid 1930s by Jerzy Smoleński[261]. It was manifested, among others, by Lemko regionalism, opposing both Ukrainian and Polish agitation[262]. Lemkos had a distinguishing set of features most strongly felt by the population: religious and cultural distinctness, and also a language that was declared by their Ukrainian neighbors to be a "broken Rus' language."[263] That language became an important differentiator of Lemko from their neighbors. As pointed out by Helena Duć-Fajfer "it is regarded as a dialect of the Ukrainian language as a rule, however, it differs significantly from the Ukrainian. In addition to the permanent characteristic accent on the penultimate syllable, in the language of Lemko there are words unknown in other dialects of Ukrainian [...] and a whole range of morphological features."[264]

The importance of the Lemko movement lies in its grassroots development and functioning. The Lemko initiative, which seeks to resist attempts to impose on them a non-Lemko national consciousness, is a factor which has been crystallizing and inspiring this group. In the desire to identify

---

[260] The aim of the "Lemko-Soyuz" was to carry out socio-economic and political work in Lemkovyna. They organized various courses in the field of household and crafts. In the field of education a reading primer by M. Trochanowski was introduced into elementary schools, which became the basic textbook to learn the Lemko language. Its press organ was the magazine "Łemko" which appeared in the years 1933-1939, see more: J. Moklak, Łemkowszczyzna w Drugiej Rzeczpospolitej. Zagadnienia polityczne i wyznaniowe..., p. 68-74; Protocols of Lemko Association Congresses 1931-1935, ed. J. Moklak, Kraków 2016; Protocols of Lemko Association Congresses 1936-1939, ed. J. Moklak, Kraków 2016.

[261] J. Smoleński, Łemkowie i Łemkowszczyzna, „Wierchy", 1936, p. 57. The passive sense of being ethnic distinction, mentioned by J. Smoleński, partly characteristic for Lemkos in the late nineteenth and early twentieth century underwent rapid changes subsequently.

[262] About the activity of the Polish state authorities in Lemkovyna see: J. A. Stepek, Akcja polska na Łemkowszczyźnie, "Libertas", no 1, Paris 1984, p. 33-47.

[263] R. Reinfuss, Łemkowie w przeszłości i obecnie. Materiały z Sympozjum Komisji Turystyki Górskiej w Sanoku z dnia 21-24 września 1983 r., Kraków 1987, p. 13.

[264] H. Duć-Fajfer, Podstawowa charakterystyka terytorialna, etnograficzna, kulturowa i religijna Łemkowszczyzny w ujęciu historycznym, [in:] Mała Łemkowyna jako region społeczno-gospodarczej aktywizacji, ed. M. Sandowicz, Warszawa 2004, p. 16.

themselves, the characteristic, as it is defined by some historians and publicists is "Lemko separatism." This is the factor around which Lemkos began to unite, and above all identify with. Ewa Michna notes that the process of shaping the consciousness of Lemkos proceeded in a manner characteristic of a borderland. Influences and desires for assimilation coming from several political centers met on Lemko territory. However, the situation in the shaping of the Rus' national movement in Galicia had a decisive influence.[265]

Probably the whole tragedy of awakening Lemko nationality lay in the fact that it began to develop almost simultaneously with the nascent Ukrainian nationalism. Moreover, Lemkos squeezed between the warring Polish and Ukrainian nationalisms were subject to different pressures, which tried to push them to adopt a particular national option. Lemko historical consciousness, understood as a common heritage and its own historical fate, played a large role in the process of self-determination. Andrzej Kwilecki, characterizing the state of the national consciousness of Lemkos before World War II, wrote that "they were a group of folk (folk society) in the phase of intensive nation-creating processes, transforming its ethnic identity under the influence of specific national groups." He emphasized that they were a group that "passed from the stage of nationality to a stage of the nation."[266]

As I mentioned, the nation-building processes taking place among Lemkos were temporarily discontinued in the years 1944-1947. After World War II the process of formation of the sense of nation took place principally on three territorial levels: the western lands (due to the number of Lemko settled mainly in the former provinces of Wrocław and Zielona Góra), historical Lemkovyna (after 1956 with the possibility of returns) and partly in the Lemko diaspora abroad (mainly in the United States and Canada).

As a result of the postwar expulsions, the Lemkos found themselves in a new and different geographical, ethnic and socio-cultural environment. In the initial period they were subjected to an assimilation process. They resulted from the general aims and objectives of "Operation Vistula."[267]

[265] E. Michna, op. cit., Kraków 1995, p. 34.
[266] A. Kwilecki, Łemkowie. Zagadnienia migracji i asymilacji, Warszawa 1976, p. 104, 108.
[267] See more: K. Pudło, Łemkowie. Proces wrastania w środowisko Dolnego Śląska 1947-1985, Wrocław 1987; S. Dudra, Poza małą ojczyzną. Łemkowie na Ziemi

Both the Orthodox Church and Greek Catholic Church had a significant impact on the preservation of the identity of displaced people. It was only in the 1950s, as a result of the partial liberalization in ethnic policy, that Lemko activists attempted reconstruction of social life, based on their own identity. This concerned both the western lands and Lemkovyna.

Until 1989, one of the main elements of the Lemko identity creation was the distancing of itself from the structures and activities of the Ukrainian Socio-Cultural Society (UTSK– established in June 1956). It is worth noting that in the initial period, some Lemkos, despite the mistrust resulting from the use of the term "Ukrainian" in the name of the Society, gave it their support.[268] Probably they pinned hopes on the possibility of obtaining permits to return to Lemkovyna, and compensation for both their material and moral losses, or to develop their own cultural traditions on new territories. However, due to the lack of a satisfactory solution for the community, in a short time there was a withdrawal from UTSK and the aspiration to establish a separate, Lemko organization. One must agree with Kazimierz Pudło that a significant part of Lemkos had their expectations disappointed because of the attitude of the UTSK's Main Board towards the Polish authorities on issues of the socio-political environment of the displaced. Since 1957 Lemkos began to gradually withdraw support from any UTSK activity, even cultural and educational ones. The general program guidelines and objectives of the Society were criticized, recognized as too minimalist and conciliatory in relation to the state. The UTSK did not take into account the primarily national aspirations of the Lemko community.[269]

An important moment in the emergence of the independent Lemko movement was a confrontation that occurred in 1957 between the Main Board and the Provincial Board of the UTSK in Zielona Góra. The latter focused largely on promoting return to the lands of south-eastern Poland. Thereby it undermined the process of stabilization of the new settlements promoted by the political authorities and the Main Board of the UTSK. It became a source of conflict and consequently the Provincial

---

Lubuskiej, Wrocław 2008.

[268] J. Albin, J. Chudy, Z genezy Stowarzyszenia Łemków, [in:] Studia nad współczesną myślą polityczną. Acta Universitatis Wratislaviensis, ed. C. Lewandowski, M. S. Wolański, no 1665, Wrocław 1994, p. 128.

[269] K. Pudło, Łemkowie, op. cit., p. 95; see more about the relations of Lemkos with UTSK: J. Syrnyk, Ukraińskie Towarzystwo Społeczno-Kulturalne (1956-1990), Wrocław 2008.

Board in Zielona Góra was dissolved. It should be emphasized that this antagonism was in some sense a dispute between two national options: Ukrainian and Lemko. It is reasonable to say that the UTSK in Zielona Góra was largely representative of the Lemko community, which strongly rejected Ukrainian national consciousness. Activists from the province of Zielona Góra stressed that this problem was very important, because the displaced came only from the areas of Lemkovyna. They said that one should not ignore the fact that part of the population did not agree to join the active work of the Society, adopting a different national option. A typical statement: "this population does not respect the UTSK; it distances itself from Ukrainians, explaining that they are from Carpathian Rus'. They consider the Ukrainian literary language as something alien and even oppose teaching their children that language."[270]

In the first period of existence (1956-1957) the Provincial Board of the UTSK sought primarily to enable those who wished to return to their homeland. Demands for the free development of Lemko culture (e.g., allowing the printing of articles in the UTSK newspaper "Nasze Słowo" in the Lemko dialect) were also put forward. In addition, branches of the UTSK focused largely on work related to granting loans for reconstruction and renovation of farms.

The above activity was determined by the Commission of the Central Committee of the Polish United Workers' Party (KC PZPR) for Nationalities Affairs as "nationalist, anti-socialist and anti-Soviet" and stigmatized by the Main Board of UTSK as "incompatible with the objectives of the Society and against the interests of the Ukrainian population in Poland."[271] This led ultimately to the suspension of the Presidium of the Provincial Board in Zielona Góra on 16 October 1957. Cancellation of provincial authorities resulted in withdrawal of other members of the Provincial Board from any activity. As a result of this situation the Provincial Board ceased to exist and was formally abolished. In the city of Zielona Góra a Society circle was organized.

The already existing inclination towards creation of an independent

---

[270] State Archive in Zielona Góra (APZG), Presidium of Provincial National Council (PWRN), Office of Internal Affairs (USW), sygn. 640, The Minutes of 4th Extraordinary Plenary Meeting of the Provincial Board of UTSK in Zielona Góra of 15 August 1957.

[271] Ibidem, Minutes of the meeting of Presidium of the Main Board of UTSK of 15 October 1957.

and separate Lemko organization began to materialize after the dissolution of the Provincial Board of UTSK. According to the reports of the Regional Office of Internal Affairs "it was likely the activities of the temporary board of the organization headed by citizens Stefanowski, Halczak and Merena"[272]. It was also stressed that the group maintained contacts with Lemko centers in the US "where they receive the press edited in the nationalist and fascist spirit, mocking and slandering the achievements of the socialist system." At the same time, the Regional Committee of the Communist Party in Zielona Góra was informed that activists from the region were in contact with the Lemkos from the provinces of Wrocław and Rzeszów.[273]

A bottom-up process of shaping the Lemko environment began in the second half of the 1950s. In the first period, it was going on among the displaced in the western lands. Lemkos from the provinces of Wrocław and Zielona Góra showed particular activity. In 1958, a "Prospective plan" referring to the Ukrainian (Lemko) minority issues was prepared in the Department for Religious Affairs of Presidium of Provincial National Council in Zielona Góra. It was emphasized that in the province of Zielona Góra "there is a tendency towards emergence of a new nationality, so-called "Lemko", from the Ukrainian minority."[274] Among the active members of this movement were mentioned Jarosław Merena, Paweł Stefanowski and Jarosław Zwoliński.[275] It should be noted that in the spring of 1956 Lemkos from Torzym (Sulęcin county) put forward the demand to "establish a Lemko organization modeled on the organization of the Ukrainian population." Among the leaders of this movement were Andrzej Zwoliński and his son Jarosław.[276] In addition, the authorities

---

[272] Ibidem, sygn. 642, The report on the issues of the Ukrainian population for the second half of 1958; about activities outside UTSK it is also mentioned in: J. Zwoliński, Rapsodia dla Łemków..., p. 75-76.

[273] APZG, PWRN, USW, sygn. 642, also J. Zwoliński describes the meeting of Lemko delegation from province of Zielona Góra with the representative of "Lemko-Soyuz" P. S. Hardy who came to Poland in 1958, among others, to organize aid for people returning to Lemkovyna, see: J. Zwoliński, op. cit., p. 91.

[274] APZG, Provincial Committee of Polish United Workers' Party (KW PZPR), sygn. 534, The perspective work plan of Group 3 of Department 3 concerning Ukrainian (Lemko) minority in 1958.

[275] Ibidem, It was stressed that the mentioned people "began to manifest their own separatism in relation to the existing Ukrainian society at the moment of making correspondence contact with the newspaper "Karpatska Ruś" and Lemko Association in the USA.

[276] Ibidem, sygn. 531, Information of the Head of Department 2 of The Provincial Of-

emphasized that "tendencies to create a separate Lemko society have been existing for a long time." In the region of Zielona Góra "supporters of such an organization are Jarosław Merena and Paweł Stefanowski." As it was confirmed, they contacted Fr. Jan Polański from Opole[277] regarding this matter. In the opinion of religious authorities, they conducted activities designed to obtain greater support among the displaced population. They propagated their views in "meetings, evenings or on the occasion of dances." Finally, the group found "many overt and covert supporters; as a result, its influence among the population began to increase and a split and division between the Lemkos and Ukrainians was clear. Some activists of UTSK stood against the activities of this group of people, especially breaking the unity of the Ukrainian minority. These disparities have led to mutual strife."[278]

Activists from the province of Zielona Góra established numerous contacts with Lemkos living in other provinces. As already mentioned Lemkos from Wrocław province played a significant role.[279] On 3 May 1958 they planned, under the pretext of a dance, to organize a Lemko convention in Głogów, aiming to establish a separate organization. Its organizers were P. Stefanowski, J. Merena and J. Zwoliński. However, due to the intervention of the Office for Religious Affairs with the Office of Internal Affairs of the Presidium of the Provincial National Council in Zielona Góra, the meeting did not take place.[280] Finally, on 25 May 1958 in Paweł Stefanowski's home in Zielona Góra, a meeting was held with a view to the establishment of a Lemko society. It was attended, among others, by Mikołaj Halczak, Jan Hrywna, Jarosław Merena, Paweł Stefanowski and Jarosław Zwoliński. During its course a Provisional National Organizing Committee of Lemkos and Rusyns in Poland was established.[281]

---

fice of Public Security in Zielona Góra of 25 October 1956.

[277] Ibidem, Information no 14 of The Provincial Commander of Civic Militia for Security Affairs to First Secretary of Provincial Committee PZPR in Zielona Góra of 15 March 1958.

[278] Ibidem, sygn. 534, The perspective work plan of Group 3 of Department 3 concerning Ukrainian (Lemko) minority in 1958.

[279] Among others Fr. Jan Polański, Emilia Janowicka, Bogdan Siokała, Maria Semczyszak, Melania Pyrcz i Marian Górski were mentioned in the document.

[280] AIPN, sygn. 051/232, About the political situation and operating environment of national minorities in Poland and tasks of the Security Service.

[281] People elected to the committee: Grzegorz Grusza, Olga Hryniak, Olga Wyszkowska, Jarosław Merena, Paweł Stefanowski, Jarosław Zwoliński, Melania Pyrcz i T. Kuziak, APZG, KW PZPR, sygn. 534, The perspective work plan of Group 3 of Department 3 concerning Ukrainian (Lemko) minority in 1958.

The objective of the Committee was to take action to return to their homes and to recognize the Lemko people as a national minority. The possibility of returning was attempted by means of a petition addressed to the First Secretary of Central Committee of the Communist Party of the Soviet Union, Nikita Khrushchev. At the same time a letter and a declaration on the establishment of the Committee was sent to the hands of Władysław Gomułka.[282] It was emphasized that the "Ukrainian Socio-Cultural Association in Poland can not in any stretch of socio-cultural life represent Rusyns-Lemkos."[283]

Lemkos' emphasizing their own identity, highlighting their separate identity, became the reason for the convening of a special meeting of the Committee of Nationalities Affairs of the Central Committee (11 August 1958), where representatives of the Main Board of UTSK, in a paper on the Lemko issue, stressed that "among the Lemko people living in the provinces of Zielona Góra, Wrocław and Rzeszów there is a peculiar phenomenon of separatism, which aimed at separating Lemkos from the Ukrainian population."[284] Further, in a distinctive tone, they stated that "a group of Lemko separatists, apparently under the influence of reactionary foreign centers, using part of the Lemko people who for one or another reason do not want to call themselves Ukrainians, want to organize a new national movement."[285]

The attempts made in the 1950s to create a separate Lemko organization were unsuccessful. This was the result of a lack of acceptance by state authorities which implemented an ethnic policy essentially recognizing UTSK as the representative of the entire displaced population from "Operation Vistula". The authorities tried to take better account of part of the demands put forward by Lemkos. An indication of this was, among others, creating within the Society a "Section for the Development of Regional Lemko Culture". The activities of this section were to

[282] Ibidem, APZG, Presidium of Provincial National Council, Office of Internal Affairs, sygn. 642, The report of Presidium of Provincial National Council in Zielona Góra on the issues of the Ukrainian population for the first half of 1958.
[283] R. Drozd, Polityka państwa wobec ludności ukraińskiej w Polsce w latach 1944-1989, Warszawa 2001, p. 160.
[284] AAN, Central Committee of Polish United Workers' Party (KC PZPR), sygn. 239/XV-140, Report at the meeting of the Central Committee PZPR for Nationalities Affairs "The issue of Lemko in total activity of UTSK in Poland" of 11August 1958.
[285] Ibidem, that reactionary foreign center indicated by UTSK was the organization "Lemko-Soyuz" from the US and its press organ "Karpatska Ruś'.

be supplementary within the functioning of UTSK, and in a sense its task was to "mute" the problem of Lemkos. The authorities of the Society took care of putting into practice its statutory tasks in the Lemko community. They demanded an emphasis of national unity with the Ukrainians. This led ultimately to the formation of mutual animosity and numerous conflicts.[286] The section developed a wide activity in Lemkovyna (especially in Gorlice district, thanks to the commitment of Paweł Stefanowski and Teodor Gocz). Its impact was smaller in the western territories. Also the supplement "Łemkowskie Słowo" [Lemko word] began to appear as a part of the "Nasze Słowo" [the "Our Word" Ukrainian language newspaper], which soon, as a result of a disapproving attitude toward Lemko autonomy, was replaced by a more modest "Łemkowska Stronniczka" [Lemko page] and then "Łemkowska Besida" [Lemko conversation]. Such activities caused dissatisfaction and Lemko activists were driven from engagement in the functioning of UTSK.[287]

Despite the unfavorable socio-political situation in Poland and the reluctance of the UTSK to recognize any manifestations of Lemko identity, further measures to emphasize national distinctiveness of this community were taken. One of its major components was the creation in 1969 in Bielanka, near Gorlice, of "The 'Lemkovyna' Song and Dance Ensemble", led by Jarosław Trochanowski. It consisted of Lemkos living both in Lemkovyna and in the western lands of Poland. In a short time, capturing and disseminating songs and dances and works of native poets and writers, the band became a durable medium of Lemko identity. The idea of annual meetings "by the fire" or "Bonfire" [*watra/vatra*], which started in 1979, has become a part of the process of the Lemko self-activity. Popular "*Watry na czużyni*" [vatra (bonfire) in exile], organized in Michałów near Legnica, later became an integral part of the cultural calendar of events promoting a wider Lemko culture.

---

[286] An indication of this was the approval only in 1963 by Main Board UTSK of the Regulations of the Section, in which they guaranteed themselves election of the section members only from the members of the Society.

[287] In addition, editors of "Nasze Słowo" often made changes in the Lemko texts sent to print, arbitrary translating them from the Lemko dialect into "the literary language", replacing the name "Rusyn" with the word "Ukrainian", changes in the spelling of words. Basically UTSK authorities and later the Association of Ukrainians in Poland (an organization created in place of UTSK in 1990) denied Lemkos' national identity, calling it "separatism" striking in the interests of Ukrainity in Poland. They only recognized Lemko ethno-cultural distinctiveness as an integral part of the Ukrainian national community, J. Albin, J. Chudy, op. cit., p. 129-133.

As a consequence of the establishment of "Solidarity" and previous Lemko activity, there was an attempt at the creation of a Society of Friends of Lemko Culture in 1982. Its initiators were Teodor Gocz, Jarosław Graban, Paweł Stefanowski, Jarosław Trochanowski and Piotr Trochanowski[288]. The Ministry of Internal Affairs was also interested in creating a separate Lemko association. It should be noted that in the information prepared about a "Lemko ethnic group" a commentator pointed out the positive elements related to the legal sanctioning of activities of such a Society. It was stated that "it would allow us to combat more effectively the ethnically Ukrainian nationalist elements using Lemko separatism. The widely known method of *divide and conquer* gives us more opportunities of appropriate programming, inspiration and operational control of nationalist elements in both environments." It was also indicated an easier opportunity "to challenge the thesis of the alleged uniformity of the minority promoted by the Ukrainian elements and to combat all sorts of initiatives such as the creation of so-called independent organizational structures for the purpose of using Lemko separatist tendencies to cause a split."[289] In 1983, the professors Roman Reinfuss and Andrzej Kwilecki were asked to take a position on the issue of Lemko ethnicity. In their opinions both professors found that Lemkos were a separate ethnographic group. In addition, Prof. A. Kwilecki added, "Personally, I have always thought that it should be made possible to create a Lemko social-cultural association. Such an association would correspond to the old traditions of Lemkos, their ambitions, referring to their historical distinctness related to residence in the Beskid Mountains."[290]

Finally, due to lack of support of state authorities and unwillingness of Ukrainian elements the attempt to create a Society of Friends of Lemko Culture failed.[291] However, in the 1980s the trend towards the development of a Lemko socio-cultural life first manifested itself and next consolidated. This refers especially to the group of Lemkos who could

[288] AIPN, Ministry of Internal Affairs (MSW) II, 7117, Information concerning the situation of the Lemko ethnic group, developed by Lt.-Col. T. Szynkowski, Major W. Sukiennik and Capt. Fr. Łucewicz of 10 December 1982.
[289] Ibidem.
[290] AIPN, sygn. 1585/6898, A letter of A. Kwilecki to Ministry of Internal Affairs of 20 April 1983, ibidem, Letters of J. Zaremba to prof. R. Reinfuss and prof. A. Kwilecki of 31 March 1983.
[291] J. Żurko, Wybrane aspekty tożsamości narodowej wysiedlonych z Łemkowszczyzny w świetle relacji pamiętnikarskich, [in:] Kultura i struktura. Problemy integracji i polaryzacji różnych grup społecznych na Śląsku, Wrocław 1992, p. 104-105.

see nation-building elements in their history, tradition and culture. This concerned both Lemkovyna and western lands (mainly centers in Legnica, Zielona Góra and Wrocław)[292].

After 1989 Lemkos acquired an unrestricted opportunity to externalize their own national aspirations in the democratizing Polish State. An important moment was the creation of the Lemko Association, the first post-war organization based on the Lemko national identity. It gathered only that fraction of Lemkos who rejected Ukrainian and Polish national consciousness, manifesting their identity and affiliation to a Lemko nation.[293] Its main aim is to integrate the Lemko people regardless of views and religious beliefs, nurturing, developing and promoting the spiritual and material Lemko culture, teaching the Lemko language, promotion of the history Lemkovyna, and knowledge about the life and activities of the Lemko people outside the country. These objectives were to be implemented, among others, by organizing cultural and educational activities (performances and review of ensembles, concerts, theater performances, lectures, seminars, exhibitions), promotion of Lemko culture and art (through the creation of libraries, reading rooms, clubs, museum and ethnographic rooms). In addition, they planned to start publishing magazines, books, brochures, to develop amateur artistic groups as well as to catalog and list monuments and relics of Lemko spiritual and material culture.[294] The press organ of this Association is *Besida* [conversation][295].

The creation of the Lemko Association was the consequence of more than century-old autonomic-ethnic tendencies taking place among the community in Lemkovyna and the recovered territories. This represented an additional element in the process of shaping the identity of this community. At the same time, it led to a deepening of divisions within the Lemko community. The consequence of this was the creation of the Lemko Union on 30 December 1989, which basically stands for of

---

[292] The manifestation of this was issuing a book of poetry by Lemko poets, among others: Władysław Graban, Petro Murianka, Paweł Stefanowski, Stefania Trochanowska, Helena Duć, or memories by Semen Madzelan.

[293] J. Albin, J. Chudy, op. cit., p. 123.

[294] Statute of the Lemko Association (owned by the author).

[295] "Besida" is an organ of the Main Board of Lemko Association. The first issue was published on 30 June 1989. Inside the "Besida" "Łemkiwska Lastiwoczka" has appeared since 1995 (Lemko Little Swallow), a magazine for children and youth. Editor of "Besida" is Piotr Trochanowski. The editorial team consists of Piotr Basałyga, Helena Duć-Fajfer, Andrzej Kopcza and Damian Trochanowski.

ethnic autonomy within the Ukrainian national community.[296] In a short time, there was a conflict between the two Lemko organizations. It was tightened after the "misappropriation" of the "Watra" [vatra] in Zdynia by the Ukrainian option.[297] Despite several meetings, they failed to build common ground. The situation worsened after the removal from power of its moderate activists T. Gocz, E. Dziadosz and T. Dubec during the First Congress of the Union.

The establishment and functioning of the Lemko organizations revealed long-dormant divisions among the community, notably regarding self-identity and self-determination. The Lemko Association created in Legnica groups that part of the Lemko population which reject Ukrainian national consciousness, whereas the Lemko Union brings together the part of this community who identifies with the Ukrainian people. The emergence of these organizations was a reflection of national circumstances bothering the community. As H. Duć-Fajfer states, the day that the Lemko Union was registered began the classic struggle between two opposing national orientations[298]. The organizational split of Lemkos created and brought to light many conflicts that emerged, among others, around the already mentioned Lemko "vatra" and the band "Lemkovyna".

---

[296] The Lemko Union was founded in Gorlice, officially was registered on 30 April 1990. The first chairman was Teodor Gocz. Its objectives were, among others, promoting the integration of Lemko people scattered on Polish territory. The Union is in favor of respecting the rights of the Lemko people regardless of their confession and how they define - as "Lemko" or "Lemko-Ukrainians". In addition, it was emphasized striving for the development of educational, cultural and scientific level of Lemkos, cooperation with all confessional communities on the basis of cultural and scientific activities. They also highlighted the need for increased contacts with the Society "Łemkiwszczyna" in Ukraine, the Organization for the Defense of Lemkivshchyna in the US, the Unification of Lemko in Canada and Rusyn-Ukrainian Union in Czechoslovakia, see: Resolution of the First Congress of the Lemko Union of 9 November 1991, [in:] Ukraińcy w Polsce 1989-1993. Kalendarium. Dokumenty. Informacje, Warszawa 1993, p. 189. It should be noted that at the congress a discussion on: who are Lemkos? was rejected, supposing that this issue had been resolved by history and is not subject to a discussion. This position sparked numerous controversies and revived anew dispute concerning the origins of this population, and above all its identity.

[297] The first "Watra" was organized as a outdoor cultural event in Czarne near Uście Gorlickie in 1982. The following "Watras" on Lemkovyna (1983-1989) took place in Bartne. They were started and run by the people who further on co-created the Lemko Association. Since the 'campfire' meetings in Zdynia in 1990 they have been dominated by pro-Ukrainian orientation supporters. The "Watra" in Michałów in Dolny Śląsk acquired strictly Lemko character.

[298] H. Duć-Fajfer, Łemkowie w Polsce, Warszawa 1991, p. 30.

At the same time, it was an expression of an existing trend in this pluralistic society.

In the 1990s Tadeusz M. Trajdos asked whether Lemkos had a chance to become a nation. At the same time, he stated that "after four centuries they have all the features and tools of culture to develop in themselves at last permanent awareness of national identity and culture. What they will be able to do, the immediate future will show. We should only wish that the creation of their own distinctiveness, reasonable and adequate, be supported by a sound knowledge of the true origins and the origin of their native community, not myths and mistaken beliefs cultivated in the futile hope that it will bring immediate political or propaganda benefits."[299]

Even during the First Congress of the Lemko Association (8 December 1990) its participants reaffirmed their desire to develop and strengthen Lemko national identity, creating the opportunity to maintain their own identity in the Polish environment for the displaced people. They also declared readiness to cooperate with all accepting their program Lemkos living both at home and abroad. In relation to the Ukrainian movement it was expected of its leaders to respect the right to freely define their Lemko national identity. At the same time they declared their willingness to cooperate with Ukrainian organizations in the popularization of the common cultural heritage and defend the interests of the whole community.[300]

At the same time the Association started a variety of activities, including, among others, in the cultural, educational, publishing and socio-political fields. An important aspect is also international activity in the general Rus' movement. In their further deliberations they paid attention to the educational aspect and activity in the Rus' movement. I believe that cultural, publishing and socio-political activities are well-known and do

---

[299] T. M. Trajdos, Osadnictwo na Łemkowszczyźnie, „Magury 90", Warszawa 1990, p. 35.

[300] During the congress the Main Board of the Association was elected. It consisted of: Andrzej Kopcza (Walbrzych) - Chairman, Piotr Trochanowski (Krynica) and Jarosław Horoszczak (Chocianów) - Vice-President, Adam Barna (Legnica) - Secretary and Stefan Kosowski (Legnica) - Treasurer. In addition, as members in the Board of Directors were: Mirosław Chomiak (Uście Gorlickie), Stefania Dubec (Michałów near Legnica), Olga Kania (Nowy Sącz), Sławomir Mołodczak (Gorzów Wielkopolski), Mikołaj Paduchowicz (Lubin) and Dymitr Rusynko (Legnica), see: Kalendarium historyczne Stowarzyszenia Łemków, developed by J. Chomiak, www.stowarzyszenielemkow.pl. [10.03.2012].

not require additional discussion.

A vital element of Lemko national identity is teaching the Lemko language. Already at the First Congress of the Lemko Association in December 1990 was announced the introduction of learning their mother tongue into primary education. In order to codify and disseminate knowledge of the Lemko language a special Committee of the National Enlightenment was founded by the Main Board of the Association.[301] On the Committee's initiative, work on a dictionary of Lemko was began at the Institute of East Slavonic Philology at the Jagiellonian University. At the same time a team to develop a Lemko grammar was appointed.[302]

The first formal post-war Lemko language education was organized in 1991 on the initiative of Mirosława Chomiak, taking place at the primary school in Uście Gorlickie.[303] Teaching also started in Kunkowa and Legnica. Later, Lemko language teaching was conducted in primary school in Krynica (1992), Rozdziele, Malczyce, Przemków (1997).[304] Currently the Lemko language is taught in twenty-three schools in Lemkovyna and in Dolny Śląsk and Lubuskie regions. Approximately three hundred students learn the language. In 2001 the Lemko language gained a presence at the level of higher education. At the Pedagogical University of Cracow, the Russian philology faculty created Rusyn-Lemko language teaching. Graduates receive diplomas allowing them to teach at schools.[305]

---

[301] Among others, the Committee of the National Enlightenment consisted of Mirosława Chomiak, Jarosław Horoszczak, Stefania Mołodczak, Piotr Trochanowski and Łukasz Woźniak.

[302] The work on grammar Lemko was guided by Mirosława Chomiak under the scientific care of Professor Henryk Fontański of the University of Silesia in Katowice. In 1992 two brochures: Gramatyka łemkiwśkogo jazyka and Łemkiwśka gramatyka dla dity were published. Intensive efforts were also taken that lead to launching the Lemko language teaching points in schools. Necessary for this purpose was the preparation of appropriate textbooks. Łemkiwśki bukwy i Leksykalne wyprawy i zabawy developed by Mirosława Chomiak and Bukwy-układanki by Piotr Trochanowski were issued in 1992. Also the pre-war textbooks: Łemkiwśki bukwar, Persza łemkiwśka czytanka and Druha knyżeczka dla narodnych szkił by Metody Truchanowski were reprintem.

[303] H. Duć-Fajfer, Szkolnictwo na Łemkowszczyźnie, "Rocznik Ruskiej Bursy 2006", ed. H. Duć-Fajfer, B. Gambal, Gorlice 2006, p. 63.

[304] Starting teaching the Lemko language was made possible thanks to Education System Act and the Regulation of the Minister of National Education of 24 March 1992 on educational activities aimed at maintaining the sense of national, ethnic and linguistic identity of pupils belonging to national minorities, Official Journal, No. 34, item. 150.

[305] M. Misiak, Łemkowie. W kręgu badań nad mniejszościami etnolingwistycznymi w

It should be emphasized that the teaching of this language has many difficulties. The principal ones are the dispersion of the Lemkos, a significant degree of assimilation of the community, and the lack of usefulness of the language in achieving social advancement.[306]

Teaching the Lemko language was made possible through curricula and Lemko textbooks.[307] Publishing activity was focused around the Lemko Association.[308]

An important element in the functioning of the Lemko Association is its activity in the Carpatho-Rusyn movement.[309] It was the initiator of the convening of a World Congress of Rusyns.[310] The first one took place in Medzilaborce (22-23 March 1991). In the course of it a permanent World Council of Rusyns was elected. It consisted of: Wasyl Turok-Hetesz from Slovakia (Chairman) and members of the Council: Andrzej Kopcza (Poland), Paul Robert Magocsi (US and Canada), Lubomir Medeszi (Yugoslavia) and Wasyl Soczka (Ukraine).[311] The Congress passed, among others, a declaration stating that "the Rusyns are not a part of the Ukrainian people, but an independent nation" and called on its members

---

Europie, Wrocław 2006, p. 123.

[306] H. Duć-Fajfer, Szkolnictwo na Łemkowszczyźnie..., p. 66.

[307] The curriculum of Lemko (Ruthenian) for primary and secondary education (1999), the curriculum Lemko (Ruthenian) for high school. The author of the program was Mirosława Chomiak.

[308] Among others, books for preschool children (Julia Prokopczak), the Lemko language grammar (M. Chomiak, H. Fontański), Dictionary of Lemko-Polish/Polish-Lemko (J. Horoszczak) were issued.

[309] See more: P. R. Magocsi, The Language Question among the Subcarpathian Rusyn, New Jersey 1987. An interesting article on the issue of the Lemko and the Rusyn movement was released by Sebastian Dubiel-Dmytryszyn, see: S. Dubiel-Dmytryszyn, Łemkowie a ruch rusiński, "Rocznik Ruskiej Bursy 2007", Gorlice 2007, p. 129-151.

[310] In addition to the Association the initiator of the congress was Rusyn Revival (Slovakia), Society of Carpatho-Rusyns (Ukraine) and combined delegations of Rusyn organizations in the US and Canada. The next World Congresses of Rusyns was held in Krynica (22-23 May 1993), Ruska Kerestura (26-27 May 1995 - Yugoslavia), Budapest (30-31 May 1997), Uzhgorod (25-26 June 1999), Prague (28- October 29, 2001), Prešov (6-7 June 2003), Krynica (27-28 May 2005) and Sigheti (21-24 June 2007 - Romania), Ruska Kerestura (4-7 June 2009 – Serbia) and Pilisszentkereszt (16-18 July 2011 - Hungary), www. stowarzyszenielemkow.pl [10.12.2016].

[311] W. Turok-Hetesz served as a chairman until 2001. Later, these functions were acted by Aleksander Zazulak from Slovakia (2001-2003), Andrzej Kopcza from Poland (2003-2005), Paul Robert Magocsi from Canada (2005-2009) and Djura Papuga from Serbia (from 2009). The World Council of Rusyns is the coordinating body of social and cultural activities of Rusyn organizations in the world.

living in different countries to work closely together.[312] One of the main ideologists of the Carpatho-Rusyn movement is Paul Robert Magocsi.[313] He introduces consistently into public circulation the term "Carpatho-Rusyn" and emphasizes that "their homeland is known as Carpathian Rus', which is located at the junction of the borders of Ukraine, Slovakia and Poland [...]. Carpatho-Rusyns are a separate nation with already formed self-awareness. They have a distinct literary tradition that dates back to the seventeenth century. Regardless of which language writers used the (Rusyn, Church Slavonic, Russian, Ukrainian, Polish or Slovak), their literary works express the essence of Rusyns' life and their mentality."[314]

A confirmation of Lemkos' belonging to the Rusyn ethno-cultural community was the speech of Piotr Trochanowski at the European Congress of Ethnic Minorities in Budapest (10 May 1991). In his paper under the emblematic title "Kurds of Central Europe" he called for recognition of Rusyns, with their own language, culture and literature, as an independent nation. In addition, he postulated that in the countries they inhabit the status of national minority should be granted.[315]

The Lemko Association hosted the Second World Congress of Rusyns, which took place in Krynica on 22-23 May 1993. It was attended by 85 delegates from Yugoslavia, Canada, Poland, Romania, Slovakia, the USA, Ukraine and Hungary. In resolutions adopted at this meeting, national recognition was requested and the granting of the status of a national minority in different countries, was proposed.[316]

The multi-directional activity of the Lemko Association is primarily aimed at promoting and strengthening the Lemko national identity. This applies to both the Lemko people living in the western Polish lands and historical Lemkovyna. Its institutionalized activity, more than twenty years old activity, has gained recognition and support from parts of the Lemko community. There is no doubt that Lemkos' tradition of having aspirations to maintain their own ethno-cultural autonomy was proclaimed by the Association.[317] These efforts were evident throughout

---

[312] J. Albin, J. Chudy, op. cit., p. 141.

[313] P. R. Magocsi, The Rusyn-Ukrainians in Czechoslovakia, "Magury 88", Warszawa 1988.

[314] P. R. Magocsi, Rusini Karpaccy, Toronto 1996 (translation H. Duć-Fajfer).

[315] It referred to the Ukrainian territory of Transcarpathia, Slovakia, The Presov Region and Lemkovyna, J. Albin, J. Chudy, op. cit., p. 141.

[316] Besida, 1993, no. 1-2.

[317] Albin, J. Chudy, op. cit., p. 143

the postwar period, but its outlet could be found only with the birth of a democratic Poland.

Lemko national consciousness has been essentially self-determined, and the whole national-creative process has been finished. The dilemma of nationality is often influenced by external factors (Polish, Ukrainian), as well as, to a lesser extent, internal ones (the question of who we are). The divided ethnic consciousness among the population raises questions about what Lemkos are today. We can agree with Tadeusz A. Olszański's statement that "they are what they believe. This means there is no reason to deny the name nation to those who think they are a Lemko nation– but also none to question the Ukrainianism of those who consider themselves to be Ukrainians." Also regarding this issue, Antoni Kroh stressed that "any historical, ethnographic, linguistic arguments may have only auxiliary value– only a sense of national unity, his or her internal option, is determinative."[318] The most important issue in this problem is to leave to the Lemkos the possibility of free self-determination and of choosing the path of development which will satisfy the life needs of this population. All residents of Lemkovyna have equal rights to this, both "Lemkos-Lemkos" [Lemko Rusyns], "Lemkos-Ukrainians", Orthodox and Greek Catholics. It is a common "little homeland" for them.

Individual decisions taken by Lemkos regarding their own national identity can not and should not be subject to external evaluations. These determinations are an inalienable right of every human being. It is worth noting that a nation is made up of people who feel that they belong to that same nation. As Norman Davies rightly noticed, "nationality is essentially a belief – a deep sense of conviction concerning one's personal identity."[319]

In conclusion, I would like to quote the words of Ryszard Brykowski: "So let Lemkos, each Lemko separately, and in a time of peace, choose their own path, which they wish, because everyone has the undeniable right to the choice to his/her own way, done with their heart or reason, or heart and reason. Let's not create any new crosses for Lemkos." And this very humanistic message should be given to all those who refuse Lemkos the right to be a nation.

---

[318] A. Kroh, Łemkowie, Nowy Sącz 1990, p. 12.
[319] N. Davies, God's Playground: A History of Poland, New York, 1981.

Church in Tylawa

CHAPTER 6

Lemkos in the United States of America

By Arkadiusz Tyda

The difficult situation of Lemkos in the nineteenth century was the main reason for their emigration. They went to the Balkans, Germany, Australia and Canada. The most common choice of destination country, however, was the United States of America. It was there that they cultivated their traditions and religion most actively. Disputes regarding their origins were carried to the United States with the Lemko immigrants, and they have continued to impact the process of shaping their social and religious life in exile. The life of Lemkos in their homeland was complicated, and a variety of issues tended to divide the community. Such heritage, for better and for worse, would leave its indelible mark on the lives of those Lemkos who settled in the "New World"[320].

Most Ruthenian [East Slavic] immigrants came to the United States between the years 1890 to 1914. Migration from Austria-Hungary peaked in the year 1907; however, ethnically Ruthenian immigration (from various regions of 19th-century Austria-Hungary and Russia) peaked in 1914, when 42,413 Ruthenians arrived in the United States[321]. Andrzej Pilch estimates that from 1850 to 1914 about 1 million people emigrated from Galicia, 90% of whom went to North America. According to him one quarter of the entire population of many Lemko villages eventually settled in North America[322].

Half of all Lemkos in the United States lived in Pennsylvania in 1910

---

[320] See: P. Matera, R. Matera, Stany Zjednoczone i Europa. Stosunki polityczne i gospodarcze 1776-2004, Warszawa 2007, p. 70.

[321] Annual Report of the Commissionere General of Immigration, Washington 1915, p. 38. The total number of immigrants from Austria-Hungary and Russia in the 1920s and 1950s was 4.172.104 and 2.242.895, F. J. Brown, J. S. Roucek, One America, Englewood Cliffs 1946, p. 636; S. Gompers, Seventy Years of life and Labor, New York 1925, s. 18-19; W. C. Warzeski, Byzantine Rite Rusins in Carpatho-Ruthenia and America, Virginia 1971, p. 96; E. T. Baranko, Carpatho-Rusyn Heritage, Detroit 1990, p. 19.

[322] A. Pilch, Emigracja z ziem zaboru austriackiego (od połowy XIX w. do 1918 r.), [in:] Emigracja z ziem polskich w czasach nowożytnych i najnowszych, ed. A. Pilch, Warszawa 1984, p. 263, 265.

(35,337). Other states with significant Lemko populations were New York, New Jersey, Ohio, Illinois, and North Dakota. Although some of these immigrants eventually returned to Lemkovyna, others moved to Wisconsin, Minnesota, Colorado, Montana, and Wyoming. Most Lemkos settled in the United States during a period of dynamic development, after the Union victory in the Civil War (1861-1865). Until the early twentieth century, Lemkos, together with Poles, Hungarians, Lithuanians, Slovaks, Czechs and Italians dominated the anthracite [coal] region. Small villages and sprawling cities such as Shenandoah, Shamokin, Minersville, Mount Carmel, Mahanoy City, McAdoo, Centralia, Nesquehoning, Lansford, Hazleton, Wilkes-Barre, and Scranton were among the first places where a Lemko community began to emerge. In the late 1890s, many Lemkos left the coal-mining regions to take jobs in the cement and shale mining industries, which were concentrated in Palmerton, Slatington, Northampton, and Catasauqua. They also took jobs in other industries: felling timber around Lopez, producing trains in factories in Berwick and mining coal or producing iron in factories near Pittsburgh. Although most joined the United States' emerging industrial workforce, others established farms around Mount Pleasant, Uniondale, Dundaff, Nicholson, and South Canaan.[323]

The most convenient destination for the new arrivals was New York, as the ships that brought them across the Atlantic touched land there. The city itself, as the largest metropolitan area in the United States, allowed them ample opportunities to find work. Lemkos also settled in the villages of northeastern industrial New Jersey. The attractiveness of this area was increased by the fact that it was also in close proximity to New York harbor. Cities such as Passaic, Jersey City, Bayonne and Perth Amboy were the first places where Lemko communities were formed, alongside the state of Pennsylvania. Many were soon attracted to Trenton because of work opportunities in the local factories and iron-steel industry. Over the next three decades, huge waves of migration from eastern and central Europe brought tens of thousands of migrants. New Jersey became the new Lemko homeland of the United States. In northern New Jersey, there were Lemko colonies in Mahwah, Rockaway and around Wharton, where they worked in the iron mines. In southern New Jersey, Lemkos lived in

---

[323] J. Davis, The Russians and Ruthenians In America, Bolsheviks or Brothers, New York 1922, p. 22-50; W. C. Warzeski, op. cit., s. 101; R. D. Custer, Carpatho-Rusyns in Northeastern Pennsylvania, Pittsburgh 2006, p. 2.

Roebling. In Manville, Lemkos worked in the glass industry. In Phillips-
burg and Alpha they were employed in the cement-producing factories.
Such cities as Bound Brook, Raritan and Dunellen became centers of
Lemko social activity.[324] During the interwar period a significant part of
the Lemko population migrated from the anthracite region in Pennsylvania to larger, more urban areas. The new centers of American Lemko
life were New York (on a still larger scale) and the other eastern cities of
Philadelphia, Pittsburgh, Cleveland, Detroit and Chicago.[325]

Lemkos, who began to arrive in North America prior to migrations
of other Greek Catholics from Galicia, consequently played a key role in
the establishment of a parish system under the jurisdiction of the Galician Greek Catholic priests. These parishes eventually formed the basis
for the creation of the Ukrainian Catholic Church in the United States.
Some churches reference the ethnic roots of their founders (St. Nicholas
in Minersville, Pennsylvania; St. Nicholas in Waterville, and St. Michael's
in Yonkers, New York). Lemkos, in the early stages of their emigration,
may thus be said to have been of key importance in the creation of Greek
Catholic parishes.[326]

The first Orthodox parishes in the US were created by immigrants
of various nationalities (with a large participation of Lemkos). With the
influx of an increasing population and subsequent to the establishment of
a parish, the Orthodox organized themselves according to ethnic origin
or language used. Churches were for them not only a place of prayer
but also a center of social and cultural life. The Orthodox mission didn't
initially help. In North America, there were no unified ecclesiastical structures nor a bishop who would have authority over all groups. Divisions
were deepened by language barriers; some of the faithful made use of
Hungarian, some Ukrainian, and some others spoke Russian. Orthodox
immigrants, including Lemkos, remained in contact with compatriots in
Europe. Thanks to a national press and [private] communications they
had an overview of what was happening in their homeland. Also, they
received first-hand information from those who had just arrived in the
United States.[327]

---

[324] R. D. Custer, Carpatho-Rusyns in New Jersey, Pittsburgh 2006, p. 2.
[325] M. B. Kuropas, The Ukrainians in America, Minneapolis 1972, p. 43; J. Davis, op.
cit., s. 31.
[326] T. E. Fitzgerald, The Orthodox Church, Westport, Connecticut–London 1995, p. 28.
[327] Ibidem, p. 34–37.

Lemko life was difficult not only in the homeland, but also in the "New World". Their hopes of quickly striking it rich and then quickly returning home were usually dashed. Their jobs quite often had a devastating impact upon their health. They worked hours above the norm, and they frequently inhaled dust in mines or chemicals in factories. The American climate frequently required adjustment, as the moist air and temperature fluctuations significantly differed from those of their homeland. First-generation Lemkos could not always afford very favorable living conditions, and as a result their houses often did not meet basic sanitary requirements. On the other hand, the next generation of Lemko immigrants would have it easier, as they could count on the help of family or friends who had already become established there. In-group community support was all the more crucial in that, due to nationality, language, religion, habits and class differences, Lemkos were largely alienated from the majority of the Protestant American society. This situation forced them to establish "fraternal societies", in which they could count on the emotional as well as economic support of other immigrants from their homeland. These groups soon began to create parishes, and later built houses of worship to suit their cultural, social, linguistic and patriotic needs. Lemkos in their parishes also began to publish newspapers. The first newspapers to feature texts in Russian, Ukrainian (albeit rarely) and English were the *Alaska Herald* and *Svoboda*. The first issue was released on March 1, 1868, and the editor was Fr. Agapius Honcharenko (1832–1916). In the articles published there, democracy and personal freedom were defended, and Russian imperialism and the conservatism and corruption of the Russian Orthodox Church were sharply attacked. In contrast, the first paper published exclusively for and by Lemko immigrants was *America*, printed in Shenandoah, Pennsylvania, in the years 1886–1890. Soon, each fraternal organization had its own magazine, with issues appearing first in their native language and then in English.[328]

The largest and most influential Lemko fraternal organization was the Greek Catholic Union (GCU), founded in Wilkes-Barre in 1892. In that same year, GCU began to publish its *American Rus' Messenger* in Scranton, which later became the *Greek-Catholic Union Messenger*. It quickly became the most influential magazine not only for the US Lemkos, but also for a wider range of visitors from [Central and] Eastern Europe. By

---

[328] M. B. Kuropas, To Preserve a Heritage. The Story of the Ukrainian Immigration in the United States, New York 1984, p. 7.

the end of World War I, it had a readership of 90,000. The fiscal policy of the organization and its tendency to identify the Lemkos as Hungarians[?], however, alienated some members. A significant part of them left the organization during the two years following its inception; they in turn created the Rusyn National Association (RNA) in Shamokin in 1894, soon to offer its own periodical, *Svoboda*[329]. Lemkos played an important role in the development of the RNA, and some of them exercised the highest administrative position. Five of the first seven chairmen were Lemkos. Due to the dominance of the Ukrainian faction, however, the organization changed its name to the Ukrainian National Association, or UNA. After this, Lemko membership in the UNA fell sharply[330].

Those Lemkos who became members of the Orthodox Church formed a pro-Russian orthodox brotherhood in Wilkes-Barre in 1895: The Russian Orthodox Catholic Mutual Aid Society (ROCMAS)[331]. Its press organ was the newspaper *Svit* (*Light*). A second off-shoot of the GCU was the Russian Brotherhood Organization (RBO), established in Mahanoy City in 1900. The RBO was founded mainly by former leaders of the GCU and RNA, subsequent to internal disagreements between pro-Ukrainian and Russophile activists[332]. Many Russophile Lemkos supported the creation of the Russian National Organization (RNO) in 1913, whose leader was a Lemko: Fr. Iosyf Fedoronko (1884–1971)[333].

Lemkos tried to cultivate their traditions in a new homeland while adapting to the new realities there. On a less pleasant note, Lemkos brought their religious and ethnic disputes with them to the United States.

---

[329] M. B. Kuropas, Laying the Foundation. Reflactions on the Early Years of Svoboda, „Ukrainian Quarterly", no. 1, New York 1994, p. 5-12; see: idem, Ukrainian-American Cytadel. The First One Hundred Years of the Ukrainian National Association, New York 1996.

[330] R. Custer, Carpatho-Rusyns in Northeastern Pennsylvania..., p. 2. Historiography of Ukrainians in North America is quite extensive, see: Ukrianians in North America. A Select Bibliography, eds. H. Myroniuk i C. Worobec, St. Paul-Toronto 1981; A. Sokolyszyn, V. Wertsman, Ukrainians in Canada and the United States. A Guide to Information Sources, Detroit 1981; O. Subtelny, Ukrainians In North America. An Illustrated History, Toronto-Buffalo 1991; M. B. Kuropas, The Ukrainian Americans. Roots and Aspirations 1884-1954, Toronto-Buffalo-Londyn 1991.

[331] http://rolandanderson.se/rocmabylaws.php [20.06.2013].

[332] Russian Brotherhood Organization of the U.S.A. Records, 1900-1993 (bulk 1919-1965) 595 boxes, 157 vols., 2 images, 223.5 lin. feet: Collection 3035, Philadelphia 2004, p. 3.

[333] B. Horbal, Iosyf Fedoronko, "Лемківскій Річник 2001", Krynica-Legnica 2001, p. 137–139.

They rapidly formed three political camps. One of them, the "Old Rus'", narrowed their ideological horizon to a shared heritage from Kievan Rus and Galicia-Volhynia. Due to the rising tensions between Poles and Lemkos (from 1848), the pro-Russian movement gained strength. Those averse to Polishness, which was perceived as a threat to Ruthenian culture, favored closer ties to Russia. This led to the formation of a pro-Russian orientation, which Prof. Moklak has termed Moscophile. On the other hand, a different faction of Ruthenians, who opposed the dominance of the Poles in Galicia, tried to open a dialogue with Polish politicians. This group viewed itself as the cultural community of Ruthenians living in the Romanov empire and created its own characteristic political ideology, called young-Russian, national or Ukrainophile. All three orientations, old-Rus', Moscophile and Ukrainophile, had supporters among the Lemko population. Their political impact only began to be noticeable in the late nineteenth century. Interestingly, Lemkos had already risen to high secular and church positions somewhat earlier; eg. Josyf Sembratovich (1821–1900) and Sylvester Sembratovich (1836–1898) had served as Greek Catholic metropolitans.[334]

Since the mid-nineteenth century, in Galicia a fierce disagreement erupted between the pro-Ukrainians, who aimed to create a Ukrainian state, and the old-Rus' party. In the eastern part of Galicia, pro-Ukrainians quickly began mobilizing almost the entire Ruthenian society around its ideology, whereas conservative Lemkovyna steadfastly withstood any Ukrainian influences.

In 1929, a group of Lemkos founded the Lemko Association (*Lemko-Soyuz*). It was a Russophile organization, although the members preferred to use the "Lemko language"[335] in their publications, thereby implicitly recognizing Subcarpathian Rus' as a separate ethnographic entity. Lemkos were called "the smallest Russian race". They used the phrase "the Russian Lemkos". The Lemko-Soyuz had a leftist orientation, pro-Soviet, but also anti-Fascist. Even after the end of World War II, leaders still treated fascism as a present threat, also strong in the US.[336]

---

[334] J. Moklak, Tożsamość Łemków – uwarunkowania historyczne (XIX-XX w.), [in:] Odkrywcy i budziciele Łemkowszczyzny. Materiały konferencyjne, red. A. Strzelecka, L. Puchała, Sanok 2007, p. 5.

[335] 50th Anniversary Almanac of Lemko Association of USA & Canada, 1979.

[336] A. Tyda, Political Activity of the Lemko Association (Lemko-Soyuz), [in:] From Political and Historical Studies, eds. S. Dudra, P. Pochyły, Stockholm 2014, p. 59.

The Lemko Association organized picnics, fairs and dancing (sometimes combined with concerts). These were usually cultural or charity events, because the intention of the organization at all such events was to raise money, either to fund the organization or its charitable activities. So as to have a full program for all these events, members of the Lemko Association formed amateur artistic groups. The branch in Cleveland had a drama club. The Circle Theatre of Yonkers usually gave a presentation at fundraising events. Similar initiatives spread to Cleveland, Passaic and Linden.[337] Performances raised questions associated with Lemko culture and the most important events of Lemko history. Political themes touched upon the injustices suffered by Lemkos in Europe. Performances were directed not only to Lemko immigrants, but also to a potentially wider US audience.

National houses served as cradles of cultural activities for members of Lemko Association. In 1938, with the participation of the Lemko Association, the Carpatho-Russian American Center was founded in Yonkers; its building was to be called Lemko Hall. The building served as the main office for the Lemko Association, featuring a lecture hall seating 300 people, the editorial offices and facilities for printing. Lemko Hall offered lessons of Lemko language and culture to its members and their families. There were lectures, theater performances and other forms of entertainment. It served as the first cultural center of Lemkos in exile.[338]

During World War II, the Lemko Association played a key role in Russian war relief by sending financial support to the Soviet Union.[339] By the end of 1941, $24,000 had been collected for this purpose. After the war, the Lemko Association expanded its activity, opening another Lemko Hall in Cleveland in 1945. The new Lemko Hall focused on serving a very active group of Lemko immigrants living in the city and offered activities quite similar to those that were well-established in Yonkers; it offered Lemko language lessons, lessons about Lemko culture, and lectures and plays.

---

[337] Лемко Союз: Кто хоче вступити въ члены драматичного кружка?, „Лемко", no. 38, Cleveland 1932, p. 1; Протокол XVIII Головного С'ізда Л. С.: Справоздание головного предсідателя В. Вархоляка, „Карпатска Русь", no. 5, Yonkers 1956, p. 3.

[338] Двадцет років..., "Карпатска Русь", no 20, Yonkers 1958, p. 1, 3; 1938-1963: 25th Anniversary Carpatho-Russian American Center, Yonkers 1963.

[339] See: E. C. Carter, Russian War Relief, "Slavonic and East European Review. American Series", 1944, no 2.

After World War II the lack of concern and interest of the European administrative authorities, the difficult financial and psychological situation of displaced people, and the lack of subsequent economic stability had a quite negative influence on the socio-cultural life of the Lemko population [in the homeland]. Local authorities shared a negative attitude toward Lemkos and treated them as second-class citizens. Direct police operations connected with "the line of Ukrainian nationalism" affected between 10,000 to 15,000 people, and about 6000 experienced active repression– including nearly 4000 prisoners of the Central Labour Camp in Jaworzno[340]. These events disinclined the Lemkos to participate in the political life of the Polish state, and they did not usually join cooperative or youth organizations. On the other hand, money and items sent from America improved the financial position of Polish Lemkos. What is more, in the US they felt free, and they enjoyed increased opportunities to organize their community.

The Lemko Association established other houses in Ansonia and Bridgeport, Connecticut. The eventual center of activities for the organization would, however, be Lemko Park– a sanatorium and resort, which was established in Monroe, New York in 1958 [at a previously existing institution.][341] One salient aspect of Lemko culture was its music. In the 1940s, Lemko bands began to record albums. Lemko Park held numerous concerts, with a May event to signal the start of summer becoming a recurrent tradition. They also formed numerous choirs. Lemko life remained very connected to their traditions, and they tried to translate as many of these as possible to the American soil. They dabbled in varying fields of art.[342] Although these efforts rarely rose to professionalism or mastery, such activities were praised, as what counted were sentimental memories and to praise the political aspirations of the organization. In the late 1960s, they began to organize larger events, and found that the demand for such performances kept increasing. One significant factor in the success of these events were the female Lemko clubs. The orga-

---

[340] Akcja „Wisła" 1947. Dokumenty i materiały, ed. E. Misiło, Warszawa 2013, p. 30–31.

[341] P. J. Best, Łemko-Sojuz USA i Kanady, [in:] Łemkowie, Bojkowie, Rusini – historia, współczesność, kultura materialna i duchowa, eds. S. Dudra, B. Halczak, I. Betko i M. Smigel, vol. II, Zielona Góra-Słupsk 2009.

[342] N. A. Cysljak, Пісни и музыка нашого народа, "Карпаторусский календарь Лемко-Союза на 1948", Yonkers 1948, p. 134-139; B. Horbal, Lemko Studies..., p. 292.

nization published several papers: *Lemko Journal, Youth of the Month, Lemko-Youth.* [From 1929 the organ/newspaper of the Lemko Association was *Lemko.* In a complicated maneuver in 1940 the title was changed to *Karpatska Rus'.*] The texts were written only in the "Lemko Carpathian Rus' dialect"; however, later they began to also publish texts in English. In its peak year, in 1945, the Lemko Association had 5,000 members in 100 branches (88 in the US and 12 in Canada). In 1945, the organization issued a publication, *Nasha Knizka* (Our Book), in which were contained the main theses of the Lemko Association ideology, the history of Lemkovyna and the issue of emigration to the United States and Canada.

Pro-Russian immigrants regularly supported their compatriots. They subsidized Mikhailo Kaczkowski's reading-rooms. The Lemkos living in Poland were also assisted by a group of older immigrants, operating from 1946 as a Lemko Relief Organization (LRO). Its leader was the industrialist Peter S. Hardy from Bridgeport, Connecticut. However, initiatives of this kind soon encountered difficulties. Neither the representatives of LRO, nor the American League of Russians and Carpatho-Russians could obtain visas to send their delegates to Eastern [Central] Europe.[343]

In America, the chief political rival of the Lemko Association was the Organization for the Defense of Lemkivshchyna in America (OOL). The rivalry between these two Lemko groups resulted from the clash of two political camps, one of them pro-Russian and the other pro-Ukrainian. The beginning of the OOL was the Central Committee of the Defense of Lemkivshchyna in America, formed in 1933 in New York with the intention "to begin to bring moral and material help to their brothers in the homeland."[344] In 1936 the Committee held a convention during which the Organization for the Defense of Lemkivshchyna was established. The Committee was then transformed into the first branch. The organization issued a proclamation which urged to make sacrifices for the homeland: "Let us all fight the enemy, and we will definitely win. In this fight let us give what we can give: financial assistance, [...] books, newspapers - educational weapon. Let us get funding for the development of our press, for poor students, for economic institutions."[345]

The OOL's members were anti-communists who supported the

---

[343] B. Horbal, op. cit., p. 291.
[344] Т. Корка, Працюйте щиро на добро свого народу й бог вам допоможе, "Лемківські вісті", no 6, Toronto 1674, p. 1.
[345] "Свобода", no 257, 1935, p. 3.

national aspirations of Ukrainians. From the very beginning of the OOL, the Lemko community in the United States that gathered around this organization was strongly pro-Ukrainian and thought of Lemkivshchyna as western Ukraine; consequently, they thought of themselves as Ukrainian. The organization grew at a rapid pace, but with the arrival of World War II it halted its activities. The reason for the loss of its authority was the suspicion that the Ukrainian community collaborated with the Nazis.[346]

The intensification of emigration to the United States in the second half of the 1940s triggered a revival of the organizations. In addition, most Lemko newcomers were pro-Ukrainian. A lot of them had been in camps in Germany and immigrated as "displaced persons". They were looking for a new home in America, but did not forget countrymen. They wanted to cultivate their tradition even away from Lemkovyna.[347] In 1957 the decision was made to renew the activities of the Organization for the Defense of Lemkivshchyna[348].

The OOL press wrote that Moscophile Lemkos had expanded the scope of their organization, publishing papers to spread propaganda in America and Europe; as such, the task of the *Lemkivskie visti* ("Lemko News") published by the pro-Ukrainian organization was to warn against this and raise the awareness of those Lemkos who had been deceived by "Moscow agents and Moscophile deceivers". *Lemkivskie visti* became the official press organ of the OOL and was published in the years 1958–1979. Developing its press capabilities had been a preoccupation of the OOL from its inception. The monthly newsletter chiefly served to spread political ideas, increase "Lemko awareness", and inform about upcoming projects. With these words, the paper outlined its goal: to criticize the Moscophile Lemkos who had thrown their lot in with the Lemko Association and published *"Karpatska Rus'"*. In the present author's opinion, such actions were most unfortunate.[349]

[346] Lemko Museum Archive, Structure of OOL, unordered collection; B. Horbal, Lemko Studies. A Handbook, New York 2010, p. 294; W. Kikta, З життя 5-ho Відділи ООL в Ірвінґтоні, Н. Дж. (1957-1992), [in:] XXIII Крайовий З'їзд: 31 жовтня – 1 листопада, 1992 р., eds. M. Duplak, W. Kikta and B. Czajkiwskyj, East Hanover 1992, p. 77-78 .
[347] Archives of the Third Branch of the Organization for the Defense of Lemkivshchyna in America (AOOL3rd), Memories of the members of OOL Branch 3, unordered collection.
[348] Відбувся величавий лемківський зїзд, "Лемківські вісті", no 5,Yonkers 1958, p. 2.
[349] A. Tyda, Political activities of the Organization for the Defense of Lemkivshchyna in

The OOL has been uniting pro-Ukrainian Lemkos for decades. Despite the difficulties facing the Lemko diaspora in the United States (e.g. the issue of cultural assimilation), the OOL's activists have made every effort to keep the memory of the Lemko community alive and to persuade them not to shed their Ukrainian national identity.

From 1965 to 1973 they concurrently released the OOL annual *Lemkivs'kyi kalendar* (Lemko Almanac). In 1979, the organization discontinued *Lemkivskie visti* and instead began publishing the monthly *Lemkivshchyna*. Members organized music bands, choirs, theatres and even a chess club (in Passaic). Lemko painter and sculptor Vasyl Madzelan lived in California, and the OOL organized exhibitions for him on the East Coast.[350]

In second and third generation Lemkos tended to move to the suburbs, which was in line with the generally prevailing trend in the United States. In the 1960s, some Lemko-Americans moved to Florida or California, looking for a peaceful abode in their old age. Despite these outliers, in 1976 the majority of Lemko-Americans still lived in the north-central states. Of the one hundred families from different cities, up to 85%, regardless of the length of their stay in the US, only moved once per generation. Lemko families usually belonged to a community that included other families of Lemko origin. Often their help had facilitated settlement in the new country, and it was subsequently often difficult to later cut the community ties they had forged. Staying together made it easier to preserve their customs from Lemkivshchyna, and moving away was usually a last resort in the face of high unemployment. The family member who got a lead about a better job in another city would usually test the waters alone first; the family would only come to join them once they felt sure they had made the right decision.[351]

At the same time the pro-Soviet orientation of the older generation of the Lemko Association members and other immigrants over time meant that many younger, often US-born immigrants underwent Russification, which identified them with the USSR as part of their pro-Russian sym-

---

America, [in:] Between Western and Eastern Europe. Political Studies: Past and the Present, eds. S. Dudra, P. Pochyły, Chicago 2015, p. 120-122.

[350] M. Duplak, Організація Оъорони Лемківщини в Америці, "Лемківщина", no 1, Clifton 1994, p. 22.

[351] J. Davis, The Russians and Ruthenians In America, Bolsheviks or Brothers, New York 1922, p. 24.

pathies. This was noticed by the new Lemko immigrants who began to arrive in the US in the 1960s. The editor of *Karpatska Rus'*, Stefan Kyczura and Teodor Dokla led a group promoting pro-Ruthenian national ideology, standing in opposition to the pro-Moscow activists.[352] Thanks to both leaders, Lemko resettlement was more directly criticized and their return to Lemkivshchyna was demanded. In the late 1960s *Karpatska Rus'* departed from pro-Communist propaganda. They also demanded raising the Lemko question in international forums, established contact with the OOL and together created the World Federation of Lemkos. Such a policy met with the opposition from older conservative members who expelled both leaders from the organization.[353]

In the times of T. Dokla and S. Kyczura many young immigrants refused to cooperate with sympathizers of Communist parties. They had been brought up in American society, permeated with anti-Communist sentiments, and it was with these that they identified, rather than with the ideology of the association of their fathers.

In 1976 the OOL established the Lemko Research Foundation (LRF), which was to take care of educational activities. The LRF is still in existence and is a non-profit organization that promotes research on the history, culture and traditions of people of Ukrainian-Lemko origin. The Foundation supports students, collaborates with academic institutions, and finances the publication of books, magazines and other materials relating to the subject of Lemkos. In the 1980s, the foundation published new editions of *Annals of Lemkivshchyna* (third, fourth and fifth volumes; the first two volumes were published by the World Lemkos Federation.[354]) LRF also released numerous books, such as *Wooden Architecture of the Ukrainian Carpathians*, edited by Hvozda[355] and *The Small Sacral Architecture of Lemkivshchyna* by T. and M. Łopatkiewicz.[356] In 2001, the most recent (sixth) volume of *Annals of Lemkivshchyna* was published, featuring texts in Ukrainian, Ruthenian, Polish and English.[357]

The OOL's most significant contribution has been the creation of

[352] B. Horbal, Штефан Кичура, "Лемківскій Річник 2002", p. 84.
[353] 50th Anniversary Almanach.., p. 10.
[354] D. Howansky Reilly, Organization for the Defense of Lemko Western Ukraine Commemorates 70th Anniversary, "Лемківщина", no 4, Clifton 2006, p. 25.
[355] Wooden Architecture of the Ukrainian Carpathians, ed. I. Hvozda, New York 1978.
[356] T. Łopatkiewicz, M. Łopatkiewicz, Мала сакральна архітектура на Лемківщині, (The Small Sacral Architecture in Lemkivshchyna), New York 1993.
[357] Annals of Lemkivshchyna (6th volume).

the Lemko Museum in 1981, which is currently located in Stamford, Connecticut. Its purpose is to cultivate and preserve the memory of the material culture of the Lemkos. The museum consists of three section: the OOL archive and those of other Lemko organizations from North America, libraries and the department of material culture, which includes thumbnails, instruments of daily use, traditional Lemko clothes, painted eggs and reproductions of Nikifor. Thumbnails were mostly collected by Ivan Honchak and are presented alongside other items from his family home, items from the church in Bartne, samples of agricultural equipment, and artifacts from working people's lives[358].

Throughout the period, Lemko cultural activity remained vital. Those scattered in the diaspora strove to preserve Lemko during the course of socio-political, religious and artistic life. The possession of a functioning organization was associated with an increase in the "prestige" of Lemkos. Having been organized with other immigrants, they no longer needed to feel lost and alone in a foreign land, as they could cultivate contacts and friendships. Many of them met as husband and wife through Lemko activism or cultural activities. The existence of organizations offered the chance to keep in contact with Lemko culture, as well as to express their political views. Depending on where they stood with respect to the pro-Ukrainian, pro-Rusyn or pro-Russian question, some Lemkos chose the organization that seemed the best fit politically. Other, less politically-aware Lemkos were guided by chance acquaintances or by which organization was more prominent in their communities; in such cases, the organization might subsequently awaken and shape their opinion on relevant political issues.

In the 1990s Polish citizens started to patronize the so-called Diversity Visa Lottery. The work involved was low-paid, often difficult and dirty, monotonous and sometimes dangerous– namely, those very jobs that Americans believed to be the least attractive.[359] Migrants did not usually

---

[358] N. Burmaka, Bulding a Lemko Museum beyond the Borders of Ukraine, "Лемківщина", no. 2, Clifton 2010, p. 14.

[359] [Unfortunately, the author of this chapter has misunderstood the USA Diversity Visa Lottery Program. Out of the one million or so visas issued for immigration to the USA, 50,000 are reserved for a lottery, that is, chance. One puts one's name in the lottery and if successful, and if one passes a security clearance, one may immigrate to the USA. Anybody can apply: lawyers, physicians, professors, dentists on one hand or on the other, farmers, street sweepers or manual laborers. Obviously, one has to be clever enough to apply so there is a tilt towards the more educated. It is meant to bring to the USA the widest selection of people from the whole planet. It is not

have much of choice among these low-status jobs, especially when they did not have the language skills for many of them. The kind of work they found usually depended upon the social networks to which they had access.[360]

After the collapse of the Eastern bloc there came a moment in which pro-Soviet connotations became embarrassing for the Lemko Association and thus it was forced to change its formula. P. J. Best maintains that after the collapse of the Eastern bloc it was too late to change the image of the association.[361] In connection with political changes in the Europe of that time, the pro-Russian orientation completely lost its meaning. Immigrants declaring themselves as Russians were put in a significant predicament.[362] The scale of the Lemko Association's events became smaller and smaller, until it almost disappeared in the twenty-first century.

The OOL didn't have such political difficulties because of its pro-Ukrainian views. The most important of the OOL's twenty-first century projects has been organizing the Lemko "Vatra" festival in the US. Because of the increasing difficulties associated with organizing smaller events, the organization focused on creating a single, larger and more general event. It was first held in 2001. The festival has taken place the past sixteen years in Ellenville, New York. During this two- or three-day event, there are concerts, lectures, and a fair, whereby important events of Lemko history are commemorated. It also serves as an occasion for Lemko activists to confer, as they attend in large numbers. It currently remains the most important manifestation of the activities of the OOL, as well as of Lemko-Americans in general. In addition, it is a good opportunity to meet with old friends. The festival serves as both a symbol of their activities and as the best excuse to meet up and maintain those traditions they had brought to the US from Lemkovyna.

Also, the Lemko Museum in Stamford, Connecticut is still open.

---

meant as a program to recruit people for low-paid, difficult jobs. — PJB]

[360] D. Stola, Kraj bez wyjścia? Migracje z Polski 1949-1989, Warszawa 2010, p. 358, 369–370.

[361] The authors conversation with P. J. Best in Słupsk in 2011; A. Tyda, Political Activity..., p. 66.

[362] P. J. Best, Cztery opcje narodowej identyfikacji karpatorusińskich imigrantów w Ameryce Północnej od późnego XIX do wczesnego XXI wieku (szkic oraz studium przypadku), [in:] Łemkowie, Bojkowie, Rusini – historia, współczesność, kultura materialna i duchowa, eds. S. Dudra, B. Halczak, R. Drozd, I. Betko, M. Smigel', vol. IV, Słupsk-Zielona Góra 2012, p. 47.

The museum is housed today in the premises of the Ukrainian Catholic Diocese of Stamford, in the same building as the Ukrainian Museum and Library. It is symptomatic that even though the museum is a unique place and still significantly contributes to the perpetuation of the culture of the Lemkos, Maria Duplak said that few members of OOL are interested in its activities. She estimated that only about 15–20% of the members visited the museum, and urged that they all must work together to ensure that the collection located there were properly preserved and given exposure, because it is an important part of the history of their community.[363] Steven Howansky also drew attention to the lack of involvement of the diaspora in the Lemko museum. He paid for the museum with his own private funds. A visit to the museum took place after a prior telephone booking, because of the rare frequency of visitors. On the other hand, it should be noted that some Lemkos engaged in the life of the museum, not just paying its continuation premiums, but also conveying exhibits.[364]

Moreover, the OOL has cooperated with many organizations of Ukrainians in the US, Canada, Poland and Ukraine: it is a member of the World Ukrainian Congress, and in the US it is a member of the Ukrainian Congress Committee of America (UCCA). The OOL representatives were usually on the National Executive Board. The OOL is a member of the World Federation of Ukrainian Lemko Associations (SFULO).[365] The OOL has taken an active part in the conferences of other organizations: Ukrainian American Youth Association (SUM), the Organization for Defense of Four Freedoms of Ukraine, Association of Former Soldiers of the Ukrainian Insurgent Army.[366] The OOL delegates have also participated in subsequent WLF Congresses.[367] Cooperation with other Ukrainian organizations exists also at the local level.

One of the biggest conflicts is about language. The Lemko Association was encouraged by the Polish *Stowarzyszenie Łemków* (Lemko Association), which maintains that Lemko is a literary language.[368] On the other

[363] M. Duplak, Марія Дупляк – голова, [in:] XXV Крайовий З'їзд..., p. 43.
[364] The authors unauthorized conversation with S. Howansky in Stamford in 2011.
[365] Cf. A. Tyda, Political activities..., p. 120–122.
[366] D. Howansky Reilly, Organization for the Defense of Lemko Western Ukraine Commemorates 70th Anniversary, "Лемківщина", no. 4, Clifton 2006, p. 13.
[367] N. Burmaka, Віддувся XXVIII Крайовий З'їзд Організації Оборони Лемківщини в Америці, "Лемківщина", no. 4, Clifton 2009, p. 27–28.
[368] M. Misiak, Łemkowie. W kręgu badań nad mniejszościami etnolingwistycznymi w Europie, Wrocław 2006, p. 25; see: Z. Sticher, Dialekt Łemków, Wrocław-Warszawa 1982; B. Strumiński, Kiedy powstał i skąd się wziął dialekt łemkowski, "Magury '93

hand, the Polish *Zjednoczenie Łemków* (Lemko Union) and the American OOL reconceptualized it as folk language, a dialect, or a cant. Lemkos generally describe it as their "family speech" and are unable to weigh in on the issue. This disagreement led to myriad conflicts and divisions among those who left during the Lemko diaspora. The official paper of the Lemko Association, *Karpatska Rus'*, described the official languages of the organization as "literary Russian or Lemko speech" and English, and the territorial sphere of its activity as including both America and "old country": "First of all Ruthenian territory of Poprad River and the Danube, the river Uzh and the San", yet also "Prešov Rus".[369] Currently the Lemko Association doesn't have any connections with Russia and the journal is non-political.

The main distinguishing feature of a culture is its language, and this is the prevalent view of Lemkos. Knowledge of the language is a source of prestige in the in-group. It facilitates identification, thus giving a sense of renewed security. It allows one to identify the language's users in today's world of internalized values. Language is one of the symbolic traits of an ethnic group. Lemkos remain a cultural group in which each element of the common culture and customs, language, religion, belief in a common origin, and the traditional material culture are co-extant with a specific, symbolic character.[370]

The Lemko language is the language of an ethnic minority remaining in a state of diaspora today. It is the language of a group that has never enjoyed statehood, as the ephemeral Lemko republics from the beginning of the twentieth century were too short-lived to have had much effect. However, in today's world, the language of a minority is no longer exclusively recognized on the basis of state or nationhood, but is also defined relative to an individual ethnic identity. A common awareness of a shared origin allowed Lemkos to preserve their ethnic identity. The most important symbol for their group identification is currently the language. Lemkos do not constitute a homogenous group in either religious or ideological terms. However, the Lemkos' attitude towards their own speech is generally positive. Today's millennial generation of Lemkos see the need to protect, maintain and promote their native ethnolect.[371]

", ed. P. Luboński, T. A. Olszański, A. Wieloch, Warszawa 1994, p. 21-26.
[369] Karpatska Rus' (1957: 1)
[370] M. Misiak, Łemkowie..., p. 69, 73.
[371] Ibidem, p. 133-134.

Among other projects, one goal is to organize meetings [dealing with culture, tradition and history].

The Lemko Association began to decline when the next generation of Lemkos became more assimilated into the American society. Increasingly, there were also problems with organizing a school where children might be taught in their mother tongue. Moreover, successive generations increasingly associated with people of various origins, rather than merely Lemkos or even ethnic Slavs, which also reflected and facilitated assimilation. Ruthenian emigrants could not easily inculcate a sense of Rusyn national identity into their children, particularly when their American leaders pigeonholed them as either part of the Slovak, Russian or Ukrainian ethnic groups.[372] Since the early 1970s, however, there has been an observable trend whereby members of the community desire to discover their roots. These are well educated Lemkos who are interested in their culture, tradition, and language. On the other hand, of the generations of Lemkos now living in the US as Americans, one should bear in mind that only a small group of them work actively in such organizations as the Lemko Association or the OOL. Furthermore, they only speak the Lemko language at home and during their meetings and festivals, especially those which are "Vatras". Parishioners' lives tend to encourage closer ties to Ukrainians, Slovaks or Russians, depending upon what community established and the trends which predominate in a particular church. Finally, once again, most relious services are now conducted in English.

Lemko organizations are not as strong as they used to be, yet they still publish journals such as *Lemkivshchyna*, with articles written mostly in the Lemko language. [Actually this OOL journal publishes in literary Ukrainian with occasional articles in English. — PJB] There are two noticeable contrasting tendencies: a pro-Ukrainian trend identified with Ukrainian culture, which is an autonomous structure of the Association of Ukrainians in Poland, as well as a second, Lemko-Rusyn tendency which rejects Ukrainianism, which has co-created the World Congress of Rusyns.[373] Paul J. Best describes the Carpatho-Rusyn orientation as currently "fashionable". He asserts, however, that few people officially own up to it. Throughout the whole of North America approximately 2000 families officially declare their nationality as Carpatho-Rusyn. The

---

[372] Ibidem, p. 78.
[373] J. Moklak, *Tożsamość Łemków...*, p. 5.

largest fraction of immigrants underwent total assimiliation in an Anglo-Saxon environment.[374]

Although Lemko membership in parishes has declined, their presence is still observable even at the upper levels of church administration. Even if it recognizes the supremacy of the pope, the Eastern Rite Catholic Church of the United States has a very complex structure, and its parishioners are very diverse. Among them Lemkos can be found. Some have risen to the top levels of the church hierarchy– for example, the bishops Stepan Sulyk and Robert M. Moskal. Others remain ordinary parishioners. The percentage of the faithful Lemkos is difficult to estimate, as they are lumped in with the total membership and often identified as Ukrainians.

Due to the enormous range of the Orthodox Church, it is difficult to assign Lemkos to one jurisdiction. However, those who decided to choose a pro-Ruthenian (sometimes pro-Russian) identity can be found primarily in the Orthodox Church in America (OCA).[375] According to Paul R. Magocsi, the Orthodox Church in America is one of the most important Eastern Christian organizations in the United States[376]; furthermore, its early growth was largely due to the activity of a Carpatho-Rusyn priest, the Reverend Alexis G. Toth (1853–1909). The US branch got its start at Kodiak Island in southeastern Alaska in 1794, where the first European settlers were Russian colonists. The word "Russian" was dropped by the former Russian Orthodox Greek Catholic Church in America in 1970.

It is difficult to determine how many Lemkos joined the Russian Orthodox Church Outside of Russia (ROCOR). It can be assumed that a significant number attended the church, yet most of these would have become completely assimilated, because the church very much emphasizes its "Russianness". Paul J. Best has personally known several members of the Russian Orthodox Church Outside Russia in the United States who are of Lemko extraction.[377]

Regarding religion services, as of the twenty-first century, in the churches the Sunday liturgy is typically held ... in English. Moreover, to continue to be attractive, churches had to adjust to the more relaxed American lifestyle. Gradually, shorter hours of worship were introduced,

---

[374] P. J. Best, Cztery opcje narodowej identyfikacji..., p. 47.
[375] Ibidem, p. 42.
[376] P. R. Magocsi, The Carpatho-Rusyn Americans, New York-Philadelphia 1989, p. 88-89.
[377] P. J. Best, op. cit., p. 42.

as well as more comfortable seating. In modern Orthodox churches, as in Catholic churches and Protestant, one finds pews. The buildings are heated, and they sometimes even have a glass partition reducing noise from families with young children. Joanna Sołowianowicz found that in the early 1990s parishes in which English was not used were extremely rare. According to her, subsequent generations of OCA faithful (that is, the children and grandchildren of immigrants educated in the United States of America) have lost interest in ethnic issues, which had become a source of problems for the Church.[378]

Some Lemkos abroad remember their own roots. The remembrance of Lemko traditions has most actively and effectively conserved by organizations which were established at the time of the very first mass Lemko migrations to Canada and the US.

To stay relevant, the church was forced to adapt... It therefore also became Americanized, since English turned out to be ubiquitous; the liturgy was abridged, and some clerics deliver their sermons almost with the conventions of televised entertainment (although such parishes remain comparatively rare.)

At present, Lemkos in the US focus primarily on publishing magazines and books (mostly historical in nature), as well as gathering from time to time for community meetings [and lectures] and to organize a "Vatra", their biggest festival. All of this testifies to the fact that their language and tradition is still alive. That said, their identity and community is clearly not as strong as it once was.

Addendum to Chapter 6

What the writer of this chapter wrote was true up through the end of 2009. However, beginning with 2010 the Lemko Association underwent a general revival when it came under the auspices of the Carpathian Institute, a project of Inter-Ed, Inc., a non-profit, non-sectarian, non-political, tax-exempt educational and charitable organization under Connecticut State and US Federal Law (a 501(c)(3) corporation under US Federal Internal Revenue Service regulations).

[378] J. Sołowianowicz, Prawosławie w Nowym Świecie, "Przegląd Prawosławny", 2003, no 9.

The Lemko Association continues to publish *Karpatska Rus'*, as an LLC (Limited Liability Corporation), now in its 88th volume year— the longest running, continuously published, Carpatho-Rusyn periodical on the planet; technically it was entitled *Lemko*, 1929-1940 and *Karpatska Rus'* 1940 to the present. Today, as a quarterly, *Karpatska Rus'* continues to cover Lemko and Carpatho-Rusyn affairs.

The Lemko Association continues the tradition of Thalerhof commemorations, held on the first Saturday of every August. Of late, Jaworzno has been added to the ceremonies. It also publishes books and pamphlets and prints maps and flags as part of its educational activities, besides organizing public lectures. The special niche today of the Lemko Association/Carpathian Institute is producing material in English, the most widely read language in the world.

The Carpathian Institute maintains contacts with the Carpatho-Rusyn Society of Munhall, Pennsylvania, the Carpatho-Rusyn Research Center of Vermont, the Chair of Ukrainian Studies of the University of Toronto, the Polish Jagiellonian, Zielona Góra and Warsaw Universities, and also the Ruska Bursa in Gorlice and the Southeast Research Institute in Przemyśl. Contacts are maintained with Prešov, Slovakia and Uzhgorod in Subcarpathian Rus'. The Carpathian Institute plays an active role in the world-wide Slavic studies organization, the Association for Slavic, East European and Eurasian Studies (ASEEES).

The reader is invited to visit the lemkoassociation.org website for current information.

Paul J. Best
General Editor
"A Carpathian Library" Series

Lemko Church in Smerekowiec, Gorlice County

Church in Powroznik

LIST OF ABBREVIATIONS

AAL - Apostolic Administration of Lemkovyna

AAN – Archive of New Acts

AIPN - Archives of the Institute of National Remeberance

APDWSz - Archives of Orthodox Diocese of Wrocław and Szczecin

APZG - State Archive in Zielona Góra

AWMP - Archives of Orthodox Metropolitan of Warsaw

BMP - Brotherhood of Orthodox Youth

GCU - Greek Catholic Union

GRN - Community National Council

KC PZPR - Central Committee of Polish United Workers' [Communist] Party

KW PZPR - Provincial Committee of Polish United Workers' Party

LRF - Lemko Research Foundation

LRO - Lemko Relief Organization

MAP - Ministry of Public Administration

MBP - Ministry of Public Security

MO - Citizen Militia [Police]

MSW - Ministry of Internal Affairs

MWRiOP - Ministry of Religious Affairs and Public Education

MZO - Ministry of Recovered Territories

NKVD - People's Commissariat for Internal Affairs

OOL - Organization for the Defense of Lemkivshchyna in America

PAKP - Polish Autocephalous Orthodox Church

PKWN - Polish Committee of National Liberation

PPR - Polish Workers' Party

PUR - State Repatriation Office

PWRN - Presidium of Provincial National Council

RBO - Russian Brotherhood Organization

RNA - Rusyn National Association

RNO - Russian National Organization

ROCMAS - Russian Orthodox Catholic Mutual Aid Society

UCCA - Ukrainian Congress Committee of America

UdSW - Office for Religious Affairs

UPA - Ukrainian Insurgent Army

USSR – Union of the Soviet Socialistic Republics

USW - Office of Internal Affairs

UTSK - Ukrainian Socio-Cultural Society

WDKP - Warsaw Orthodox Spiritual Consistory

LIST OF SOURCES AND LITERATURE

Archival sources

Archives of New Acts
Archive of the Institute of National Remembrance
State Archive in Rzeszów
State Archive in Zielona Góra
Archives of the Orthodox Metropolitan of Warsaw
Archives of the Orthodox Diocese of Wrocław and Szczecin

Published source materials

Akcja „Wisła". Dokumenty, ed. E. Misiło, Warszawa 2013

Annual Report of the Commissioner General of Immigration, Washington 1915

Repatriacja czy deportacja. Przesiedlenie Ukraińców z Polski do USRR 1944-1946. Dokumenty 1944-1945, vol. 1, ed. E. Misiło, Warszawa 1996.

Duchowni greckokatoliccy i prawosławni w Centralnym Obozie pracy w Jaworznie (1947-1949). Dokumenty i materiały, ed. I. Hałagida, Warszawa 2012

Memoirs

W. Sahajdakiwśkyj, *Prawdy ne wtopyty. Spohady z 50-tyriczczia pasterstwa 1927-1977*, Toronto 1977

Press

"Antyfon"
"Cerkownyj Kalendar"
"Cerkiewny Wiestnik"
"Лемківскій Річник"
"Лемківські вісті"
"Лемко"
"Лемківщина"

"Magury"
"Карпатска Русь"
"Карпаторусский календар Лемко-Союза на 1948"
"Przegląd Prawosławny"
"Slavonic and East European Review. American Series"
"Свобода"
"Tygodnik Powszechny"
"Ukrainian Quarterly"
"Wiadomości PAKP"
"Życie Literackie"

Studies

Akcja „Wisła", ed. J. Pisuliński, Warszawa 2003

Baranko E.T., *Carpatho-Rusyn Heritage, Detroit 1990*

Barna A., *Kronika-Litopis żytia religijno-gromadiańskogo parafii seła Czorne na Lemkowyni 1770-1970, Legnica 1997*

Bendza M., *Prawosławna diecezja przemyska w latach 1596-1681. Studium historyczno-kanoniczne, Warszawa 1982*

Best P. J., *Cztery opcje narodowej identyfikacji karpatorusińskich imigrantów w Ameryce Północnej od późnego XIX do wczesnego XXI wieku (szkic oraz studium przypadku), [in:] Łemkowie, Bojkowie, Rusini – historia, współczesność, kultura materialna i duchowa, eds. S. Dudra, B. Halczak, R. Drozd, I. Betko, M. Smigel', vol. IV, 1, Słupsk-Zielona Góra 2012*

Bołtryk M., *Sąd nad Świętym Maksymem, Gorlice 2014.*

Brown F. J., *J. S. Roucek, One America, Englewood Cliffs 1946*

Burski J. J., *A. Nowak, Wyznaniowe wczoraj i dziś Łemkowszczyzny, „Rocznik Ruskiej Bursy", 2005, ed. H. Duć-Fajfer, B. Gambal, Gorlice 2005*

Charkiewicz J., *Bractwo Młodzieży Prawosławnej w Polsce, Białystok 1995*

Charkiewicz J., *Męczennicy XX wieku. Martyrologia prawosławia w Polsce w biografiach świętych, Warszawa 2004*

Custer R.D., *Carpatho-Rusyns in Northeastern Pennsylvania, Pittsburgh 2006*

Czajkowski J., *Studia nad Łemkowszczyzną, Sanok 1999*

Davies N., *God's playground: a history of Poland, Oxford 2005*

Davis J., *The Russians and Ruthenians In America, Bolsheviks or Brothers, New York 1922*

Dobrowolski K., *Migracje wołoskie na ziemiach polskich, Lwów 1930*
Drozd R., *Polityka państwa wobec ludności ukraińskiej w Polsce w latach 1944-1989, Warszawa 2001*
Dubec R., *Proces odradzania się Kościoła prawosławnego na Łemkowszczyźnie w okresie międzywojennym, "Almanach Diecezjalny 2006", vol. 2, Gorlice 2006*
Dubec R., *Recepcja św. Maksyma Gorlickiego w Polsce i na świecie, "Almanach Diecezjalny" 2005, Gorlice 2006, vol. 1*
Dubiel-Dmytryszyn S., *Łemkowie a ruch rusiński, „Rocznik Ruskiej Bursy 2007", Gorlice 2007*
Duć-Fajfer H., *Łemkowie w Polsce, "Magury 91"*
Duć-Fajfer H., *Literatura łemkowska w drugiej połowie XIX i na początku XX wieku, Kraków 2001*
Duć-Fajfer H., *Szkolnictwo na Łemkowszczyźnie, "Rocznik Ruskiej Bursy 2006", ed. H. Duć-Fajfer, B. Gambal, Gorlice 2006*
Dudra S., *Cerkiew w diasporze. Z dziejów prawosławnej diecezji wrocławsko-szczecińskiej, Poznań 2009*
Dudra S., *Cerkiew w Polanach. Z dziejów konfliktu wyznaniowego na Łemkowszczyźnie, "Rocznik Ruskiej Bursy 2009", Gorlice 2009*
Dudra S., *Poza małą ojczyzną. Łemkowie na Ziemi Lubuskiej, Wrocław 2008*
Emigracja z ziem polskich w czasach nowożytnych i najnowszych, *ed. A. Pilch, Warszawa 1984*
Ergetowski R., *Poczajowska Ławra, "Wrocławskie Studia Wschodnie", 2005, no 9*
Fastnach A., *Osadnictwo ziemi sanockiej w latach 1340-1650, Wrocław 1962*
Fitzgerald T. E., *The Orthodox Church, Westport, Connecticut–London 1995*
Gerent P., *Prawosławie na Dolnym Śląsku w latach 1945-1989, Toruń 2007*
Gerent P., *Zarys dziejów prawosławnej diecezji przemyskiej, "Almanach Diecezjalny", 2005, vol. 1, Gorlice 2005*
Gompers S., *Seventy Years of life and Labor, New York 1925*
Hajduczenia O., *Wychowawcze oddziaływanie wybranych form działalności Bractwa Młodzieży Prawosławnej, Białystok 1990*
Hałagida I., *Między Moskwą, Warszawą i Watykanem. Dzieje Kościoła greckokatolickiego w Polsce w latach 1944-1970, Warszawa 2013.*
Historia martyrologii więźniów obozów odosobnienia w Jaworznie

1939-1956, *ed. K. Miroszewski i Z. Woźniczka, Jaworzno 2002*

Horbal B., *Lemko Studies: A Handbook, New York 2010.*

Ikony cerkwi prawosławnej w Brzozie, *Strzelce Krajeńskie 2005.*

Inwentaryzacja łemkowskich cmentarzy w nieistniejących wsiach na terenie gminy Sękowa. part 1. Banica, *Długie, Lipna (stan na 31.10.2002)", ed. R. Dubec, Gorlice 2003*

Jaworzno. Spohady wjazniw polśkoho koncentracijnoho taboru, *ed. B. Huk, M. Iwanyk, Peremyszl-Toronto-Lwiw 2007*

Kultura i struktura. Problemy integracji i polaryzacji różnych grup społecznych na Śląsku, *Wrocław 1992*

Kuprianowicz G., *Prawosławnaja Cerkwa na Chołmszczyzni, Piwdennom Pidliaszi i Lemkowszczini w 40 roki XX st. i akcja „Wisła", "Cerkiewny Wiestnik", 2002, no 3.*

Kuropas M. B., *To Preserve a Heritage. The Story of the Ukrainian Immigration in the United States, New York 1984*

Kuropas M. B., *Ukrainian-American Cytadel. The First One Hundred Years of the Ukrainian National Association, New York 1996*

Kuropas M.B., *The Ukrainian Americans. Roots and Aspirations 1884-1954, Toronto-Buffalo-Londyn 1991*

Kuropas M.B., *The Ukrainians in America, Minneapolis 1972*

Kwiek J., *Żydzi, Łemkowie, Słowacy w województwie krakowskim w latach 1945-1949/50, Kraków 1998*

Kwilecki A., *Fragmenty najnowszej historii Łemków (ze szczególnym uwzględnieniem Łemków sądeckich), "Rocznik Sądecki", 1967, vol. VIII,*

Kwilecki A., *Łemkowie. Zagadnienie migracji i asymilacji, Warszawa 1974*

Kwilecki A., *Problemy socjologiczne Łemków na Ziemiach Zachodnich, "Kultura i Społeczeństwo", 1966, no 3*

Kwilecki A., *Zagadnienia stabilizacji Łemków na Ziemiach Zachodnich, "Przegląd Zachodni", 1966, no 6*

Lemkin I. F., *Istorija Lemkowyny, Yonkers, N.Y. 1969*

Łemkowie w historii i kulturze Karpat, *red. J. Czajowski, Rzeszów 1992*

Łemkowie, *Bojkowie, Rusini. Historia, współczesność, kultura materialna i duchowa, ed. S. Dudra, B. Halczak, A. Ksenicz, J. Starzyński, Legnica-Zielona Góra 2007*

Łemkowie. Historia i kultura. Sesja naukowa Szreniawa 30 czerwca-1 lipca 2007, *Szreniawa 2007*

Łesiów M., *Rola kulturotwórcza Ukraińskiej Cerkwi Greckokatolickiej, Lublin 2001*

Lewicki J., *Grammatik der ruthenischen oder kleinrussichen Sprache in Galizien, Przemyśl 1834.*

Łopatkiewicz T., M. *Łopatkiewicz, Мала сакральна архітектура на Лемківщині, (The Small Sacral Architecture in Lemkivshchyna), New York 1993*

Magocsi P.R., *The Carpatho-Rusyn Americans, New York-Philadelphia 1989*

Magocsi P.R., *The Rusyn-Ukrainians in Czechoslovakia, "Magury 88", Warszawa 1988*

Mała Łemkowyna jako region społeczno-gospodarczej aktywizacji, *ed. M. Sandowicz, Warszawa 2004*

Maryański A., *Migracje w świecie, Warszawa 1984*

Matera P., *R. Matera, Stany Zjednoczone i Europa. Stosunki polityczne i gospodarcze 1776-2004, Warszawa 2007*

Michalak R., *Polityka wyznaniowa państwa polskiego wobec mniejszości religijnych w latach 1945-1989, Zielona Góra 2014.*

Michna E., *Łemkowie. Grupa etniczna czy naród, Kraków 1995*

Misiak M., *Łemkowie. W kręgu badań nad mniejszościami etnolingwistycznymi w Europie, Wrocław 2006*

Misiło E., *Pawłokoma 3 III 1945, Warszawa 2006*

Moklak J., *Kształtowanie się struktury Kościoła prawosławnego na Łemkowszczyźnie w Drugiej Rzeczypospolitej, "Magury 97"*

Moklak J., *Łemkowszczyzna w Drugiej Rzeczypospolitej. Zagadnienia polityczne i wyznaniowe, Kraków 1997*

Motyka G., *Tak było w Bieszczadach. Walki polsko-ukraińskie 1943-1948, Warszawa 1999*

Nalepa J., *Łemkowie, Wołosi i Biali Chorwaci. Uwagi dotyczące kwestii genezy osadnictwa na polskim Podkarpaciu, "Acta Archeologica Carpathia", 1997-1998, vol. 34*

Obóz dwóch totalitaryzmów – Jaworzno 1943-1956, *ed. R. Terlecki, Jaworzno 2007, vol. 2*

Odkrywcy i budziciele Łemkowszczyzny. Materiały konferencyjne, *red. A. Strzelecka, L. Puchała, Sanok 2007*

Olszański T. A., *Drogi tożsamości Łemków, "Magury 90", Warszawa 1990*

Olszański T. A., *Geneza Łemków – teorie i wątpliwości, "Magury 88", Warszawa 1988*

Olszański T. A., *Z dziejów Kościoła na Łemkowszczyźnie, "Chrześcijanin w Świecie", no 179-180, Warszawa 1988*

Opowieści z Brzozy i okolic, *part. 2, Strzelce Krajeńskie 2004*

Osadczy W., *Święta Ruś. Rozwój i oddziaływanie idei prawosławia w Galicji, Lublin 2007*

Pamiętny rok 1947, *ed. M. E. Ożóg, Rzeszów 2001*

Pawluczuk U. A., *Życie monastyczne w II Rzeczypospolitej, Białystok 2007*

Pisuliński J., *Przesiedlenia ludności ukraińskiej z Polski do USSR w latach 1944-1947, Rzeszów 2009*

Podlaski K., *Białorusini-Litwini-Ukraińcy, Londyn 1985*

Pol W., *Rzut oka na północne stoki Karpat, Kraków 1851.*

Polska-Ukraina 1000 lat sąsiedztwa, *ed. S. Stępień, vol. III, Przemyśl 1996*

Polska-Ukraina 1000 lat sąsiedztwa, *vol. 1, Przemyśl 1990*

Polska-Ukraina spotkanie kultur. Materiały z sesji naukowej, *ed. T. Stegner, Gdańsk 1997.*

Problemy Ukraińców w Polsce po wysiedleńczej akcji „Wisła" 1947 roku, *ed. W. Mokry, Kraków 1997*

Protocols of Lemko Association Congresses 1931-1935, *ed. J. Moklak, Kraków 2016*

Protocols of Lemko Association Congresses 1936-1939, *ed. J. Moklak, Kraków 2016.*

Pudło K., *Łemkowie, Proces wrastania w środowisko Dolnego Śląska 1947-1985, Wrocław 1987*

Radziukiewicz A., *M. Bołtryk, Precz z mnichami, Białystok 1995*

Reinfuss R., *Łemkowie jako grupa etnograficzna, Sanok 1998*

Reinfuss R., *Łemkowie w przeszłości i obecnie. Materiały z Sympozjum Komisji Turystyki Górskiej w Sanoku z dnia 21-24 września 1983 r., Kraków 1987*

Reinfuss R., *Śladami Łemków, Warszawa 1990*

Rożko W., *Peczerni monastyri Wołyni i Polissia, Łuck 2008.*

Rusynko D., *A. Barna, Piorunka-Perunka i jej mieszkańcy, Legnica 2007*

Ryńca M., *Administracja Apostolska Łemkowszczyzny w latach 1945-1947, Kraków 2003*

Smoleński J., *Łemkowie i Łemkowszczyzna, "Wierchy", R. XIV, 1936*

Sokolyszyn A., *V. Wertsman, Ukrainians in Canada and the United States. A Guide to Information Sources, Detroit 1981*

Sosna G., *A. Troc-Sosna, Hierarchia i duchowieństwo Kościoła prawosławnego w granicach II Rzeczypospolitej i Polski powojennej w XIX i XXI wieku, Ryboły 2012*

Stepek J. A., *Akcja polska na Łemkowszczyźnie, „Libertas", no 1, Paris 1984*

Sticher Z., *Dialekt Łemków, Wrocław-Warszawa 1982*

Stieber Z., *Wschodnia granica Łemków, "Sprawozdania z Czynności i Posiedzeń PAU", 1935, vol. 40, no 8*

Stola D., *Kraj bez wyjścia? Migracje z Polski 1949-1989, Warszawa 2010*

Subtelny O., *Ukrainians In North America. An Illustrated History, Toronto-Buffalo 1991*

Sulimirski T., *Trakowie w północnych Karpatach i problem pochodzenia Wołochów, "Magury 85", Warszawa 1985*

Syrnyk J., *Ukraińskie Towarzystwo Społeczno-Kulturalne (1956-1990), Wrocław 2008*

Szafarzyk P., *Slovanskie Starożitnosty, Praha 1837*

Szanter Z., *Osadnictwo z południa w Beskidzie Niskim i Sądeckim, "Polska Sztuka Ludowa", XXXIX, no 3-4, Warszawa-Wrocław 1985*

    Szanter Z., *Skąd przybyli przodkowie Łemków? O osadnictwie z południowych stoków Karpat w Beskidzie Niskim i Sądeckim, "Magury 93"*

Szemłej J., *Z badań nad gwarą łemkowską, "Lud Słowiański", 1934, vol. 3, part. 2*

Szkarowskij M. W., *Nacistkaja Germania i Prawosławnaja Cerkow (Nacistkaja politika w odnoszenii Prawosławnoj Cerkwi i religioznoje wozrożdennie na okupowannoi teritorii CCCP), Moskwa 2002*

Trajdos T. M., *Osadnictwo na Łemkowszczyźnie, "Magury 90", Warszawa 1990*

Trochanowski P., *Postać Świętego Maksyma w twórczości literackiej, "Almanach Diecezjalny", 2005, vol. 1*

Trochanowski P., *Wertania z rozdilenych dorich, "Cerkownyj Kalendar", 1987*

Truchan M., *Nehatywnyj stereotyp Ukrajincia w polskij literaturi, Monachium-Lwów 1992*

Truchan M., *Ukrajinci w Polszczi pislia druhoji switowoji wijny 1944-1984, Nowy York 1990*

Tyda A., *Political activities of the Organization for the Defense of Lemkivshchyna in America, [in:] Between Western and Eastern Europe. Political Studies: Past and the Present, eds. S. Dudra, P. Pochyły, Chicago 2015*

Tyda A., *Political Activity of the Lemko Association (Lemko-Soyuz), [in:] From Political and Historical Studies, eds. S. Dudra, P. Pochyły, Stockholm 2014*

U poszukach prawdy pro akciju „Wisła", *ed. M. Kozak, Peremyszl 1998*

144 *Stefan Dudra*

Udziela S., *Rozsiedlanie się Łemków, "Wisła", 1889, vol. 3*

Ukrajina i Polszcza miż mynułym i majbutnym, *Lwiw 1991*

Ukrianians in North America. A Select Bibliography, *eds. H. Myroniuk i C. Worobec, St. Paul-Toronto 1981*

Urban K., *Kościół prawosławny w Polsce 1945-1970 (rys historyczny), Kraków 1996*

Urban K., *Ks. Stefan Biegun (1903-1983). Zapis jednego życia, Kraków 2000*

Urban K., *Z dziejów Kościoła prawosławnego na Łemkowszczyźnie w latach 1945-1947, "Zeszyty Naukowe Akademii Ekonomicznej w Krakowie", no 460, Kraków 1995*

Warzeski, W.C., *Byzantine Rite Rusins in Carpatho-Ruthenia and America, Virginia 1971*

Własowśkyj I., *Narys istorii Ukrainśkoj Prawosławnoji Cerkwy, vol. IV, part 2, New York 1993*

Wojewoda Z., *Zarys historii Kościoła greckokatolickiego w Polsce w latach 1944-1989, Kraków 1994*

Wooden Architecture of the Ukrainian Carpathians, *ed. I. Hvozda, New York 1978.*

Wójtowicz-Huber B., *Ojcowie narodu. Duchowieństwo greckokatolickie w ruchu narodowym Rusinów galicyjskich (1867-1918), Warszawa 2008*

Wolski K., *Stan polskich badań nad osadnictwem wołoskim na północ od Karpat, "Rocznik Przemyski", 1958*

Wooden Architecture of the Ukrainian Carpathians, *ed. I. Hvozda, New York 1978*

Wyrwich M., *Łagier Jaworzno. Z dziejów czerwonego terroru, Warszawa 1995*

XXIII Крайовий З'їзд: 31 жовтня – 1 листопада, *1992 p., eds. M. Duplak, W. Kikta and B. Czajkiwskyj, East Hanover 1992*

Z łemkowskiej skrzyni. Opowieści z Ługów i okolic, *part. 1, Strzelce Krajeńskie 2003*

Z myślą o Polsce Ludowej, *Rzeszów 1963*

Zwoliński J., *J. Merena, Na Łemkowszczyźnie. Floryna (nasze seło), Koszalin 1999*

Zwoliński J., *Rapsodia dla Łemków, Koszalin 1994*

Żak J., *A. Piecuch, Łemkowskie cerkwie, Warszawa 2011*

Index

A CARPATHIAN LIBRARY

This collection of materials deals with the Slavic inhabitants of the Carpathian Mountains of Central and their descendants wherever found.

ENGLISH

1. *The Lemkos: Articles and Essays* (second edition, revised and expanded), edited by Paul Best and Jaroslaw Moklak, Carpathian Institute, 2016, 300 pages. This publication contains papers and related materials from conferences in the 1990s and the 21st century. $25.00

2. *The Lemko Region, 1939-1947: War, Occupation and Deportation*, edited by Paul Best and Jaroslaw Moklak, The Lemko Association and the Carpathian Institute, 2002, 280 pages. Selected papers from a conference at the Jagiellonian University in 2001 and materials from other sources.
.... $25.00

3. *Does a Fourth Rus' Exist?: Concerning Cultural Identity in the Carpathian Region*, edited by Paul Best and Stanislaw Stepien, Przemysl-Higganum, 2009, 200 pages $25.00

4. *Lemkovyna: A History of the Lemko Region of the Carpathian Mountains of Central Europe,* by Father Ioann Polianskii (writing as I.F. Lemkyn), translated and edited by Paul Best, Michael Decerbo and Walter Maksimovich, Carpathian Institute, 2012. This is a translation of the Lemko language history by Polianskii listed below.Paperback $20.00, hardbound $30.00

5. Simeon Pyzh's *A Short History of Carpathian Rus'*, translated Andrew Yurkovsky and Paul Best, edited by Paul Best and Michael Decerbo, Carpathian Institute, 2016, This short book is not only a translation but also includes the original text. Hardbound $20.00

LEMKO

6. *История Лемковины в 5 Частях* (The history of Lemkovyna in 5 parts), I. F. Lemkin (Fr. Ioann Polianskii), Yonkers, New York, 1969, The Lemko Association, 384 pages, with photos and illustrations. This is a Lemko language history of the region written by a patriotic Greek Catholic priest. $15.00

RUSSIAN

The Carpathian Institute also offers the Peter and Anastasia collection of Russophile materials, reprints of Russian language books published in the late 19th and early 20th centuries. These materials support the idea that all of East Slavdom (Russia, Ukraine, Belarus, Carpathian Rus') form a single unified whole.

These books, along with maps, flags, brochures and pamphlets may be purchased from:

The Carpathian Institute
184 Old County Road
Higganum, Connecticut 06441-4446
USA
telephone: 1-860-345-7997
fax: 1-860-345-3598
email: merida@snet.net
website: lemkoassociation.org

www.ingramcontent.com/pod-product-compliance
Lightning Source LLC
Chambersburg PA
CBHW072115090426
42739CB00012B/2974